CW00530330

Dangerous Minds

Dangerous Minds

Nietzsche, Heidegger, and the Return of the Far Right

Ronald Beiner

PENN

UNIVERSITY OF PENNSYLVANIA PRESS

PHILADELPHIA

Published by
University of Pennsylvania Press
Philadelphia, Pennsylvania 19104-4112
www.upenn.edu/pennpress

Printed in the United States of America

A Cataloging-in-Publication record is available from the Library of
Congress

ISBN 978-0-8122-5059-6

In memory of Howard Tessler

Contents

Introduction

Nietzschean Ideologies in the Twenty-First Century

> Eleven pass, and then
> Athene takes Achilles by the hair,
> Hector is in the dust, Nietzsche is born,
> Because the hero's crescent is the twelfth.
> —Y. B. Yeats, "The Phases of the Moon"

In the fateful fall of 2016, a far-right ideologue named Richard B. Spencer stirred up some fame for himself by exclaiming to a conference room packed with his followers not far from the White House: "Hail Trump! Hail our people! Hail victory!" On the face of it, this mad proclamation would appear to have nothing in common with the glorious tradition of Western philosophy. Yet consider a few other provocative remarks ventilated by Spencer: "American society today is so just fundamentally bourgeois. It's just so, pardon my French . . . it's so fucking middle class in its values. There is no value higher than having a pension and dying in bed. I find that profoundly pathetic. So, yeah, I think we might need a little more chaos in our politics, we might need a bit of that fascist spirit in our politics."[1] Or consider this quote from Spencer in a profile by Sarah Posner in the October 18, 2016, issue of *Rolling Stone*: "I love empire, I love power, I love achievement." Posner reports that "Spencer loves imperialism so much, he says, that he'll sometimes 'get a boner' reading about Napoleon."[2] There is no question about the Nietzschean lineage of these sentiments. Spencer knows that they're Nietzschean, and any honest reader of Nietzsche knows that they're Nietzschean.

Or consider Spencer's ideological kinsman, Russia's far-right political thinker Aleksandr Dugin. In April 2014, Dugin participated in an hour-long interview with Russian television host Vladimir Posner. Near the end of the show, Posner asked Dugin, "Is there a philosophical quote that is especially dear to you?" Dugin responded, "Yes: man is something that should be overcome."[3] Dugin didn't specify the source of this "especially dear" quote—probably because it would have revealed something of a tension with Dugin's strongly avowed adherence to Orthodox Christianity of the Old Believer variety. But he didn't need to specify the source—anyone with any acquaintance with *Thus Spoke Zarathustra* knows that it's Nietzsche. Anton Shekhovtsov, a commentator on Dugin, quotes an essay in which Dugin presents himself as a prophet of a "new aeon" that "will be cruel and paradoxical," involving slavery, "the renewal of archaic sacredness," and "a cosmic rampage of the Superhuman." Similarly, Shekhovtsov quotes another Dugin text affirming a vision of fascism that promises "to give birth to a society of the hero and Superhuman."[4] Dugin is part Old

Believer, part Nietzschean, part occultist, part bohemian, part warlord, part guru, part geopolitical strategist, and part plain maniac. (He's the postmodern subject par excellence!)[5]

Inhabiting the same murky swamp is Julius Evola, the monocled baron, Italian exponent of über-fascism, and an explicit disciple of Nietzsche. Charles Clover, in an illuminating recent book on Dugin and his ideological forebears, gives a helpful glimpse into Evola's vision of caste-based Nietzschean neoaristocracy: "He believed that war was a form of therapy, leading mankind into a higher form of spiritual existence."[6] Another striking dictum of Dugin's worth pondering is the following, as recorded in the interview cited in the previous paragraph: "The essence of the human being is to be a soldier."[7] Such views capture quite well why the thinkers expressing these views are committed, in a faithfully Nietzschean spirit, to the root-and-branch rejection of the way of life embodied in liberal, bourgeois, egalitarian societies.

Doug Saunders, a thoughtful Canadian journalist, wrote the following in the February 11, 2017, issue of *The Globe and Mail*: "Europe's far-right parties have been ushered into prominence . . . by a flood of bestsellers with titles such as *Germany Abolishes Itself*; *The Last Days of Europe*; *After the Fall: The End of the European Dream and the Decline of a Continent*; *Reflections on the Revolution in Europe*; *Decline and Fall: Europe's Slow-Motion Suicide*; and *Submission*. All argue that a weakened, feminized, coddled, birth-controlled Western culture has become too soft and impassive to resist invasion and dominance by supposedly more muscular, more fertile, and more aggressive Asian and Islamic cultures." It would not be a difficult task to show that the original source of this rhetoric is traceable back to Nietzsche.[8]

One of the truly great mysteries of twentieth- (and now twenty-first-) century intellectual life is how a thinker as forthrightly and bluntly antiegalitarian and antiliberal as Friedrich Nietzsche could have become pretty much the most influential philosopher of the twentieth century (a phenomenon then replicated by a philosophical successor no less antiegalitarian and antiliberal—namely, Martin Heidegger). The intellectual influence of Nietzsche is of staggering breadth—not least within the precincts of the intellectual and cultural left. The solution of this puzzle will probably be left to sociologists of knowledge fifty or a hundred years from now. In the meantime, however, we must do our best to weigh the intellectual power of Nietzsche while at the same time fully appreciating the dangerousness or possible perils of that intellectual power. The same goes for Heidegger.

Friedrich Nietzsche once wrote the following: "The great majority of men have no right to life, and serve only to disconcert the elect among our race; I do not yet grant the unfit that right. There are even unfit peoples."[9] Martin Heidegger once wrote the following:

> An enemy is each and every person who poses an essential threat to the Dasein [existence] of the people and its individual members. The enemy does not have to be external, and the external enemy is not even always the more dangerous one. And it can seem as if there were no enemy. Then it is a fundamental requirement to find the enemy, to expose the enemy to the

light, *or even first to make the enemy*, so that this standing against the enemy may happen and so that Dasein
may not lose its edge. . . . [The challenge is] to bring the
enemy into the open, to harbor no illusions about
the enemy, to keep oneself ready for attack, to cultivate and intensify a constant readiness and to pre-
pare the attack *looking far ahead with the goal of total
annihilation.*[10]

These are both incitements to genocide. The point of
quoting these statements is not to impugn Nietzsche and
Heidegger as important thinkers. Nietzsche was a great
philosopher. Heidegger was a great philosopher. Nothing
in this book is meant to challenge their intellectual stature.
There's no intention here to expel them from the history of
philosophy (as there is in Emmanuel Faye's severely critical work on Heidegger). But they are not innocent. Great
thinkers can be dangerous thinkers. And to the extent that
their ideas contribute to bad ideological currents in the
present, we have to be alert to their noninnocence and do
our utmost not to become their apologists. We need to
commence a serious engagement with Nietzsche and
Heidegger because, in the end, these thinkers are not the
resources for the left that we have so often been told that
they are. In a longer-term view, they are more likely to be
resources for the right and far right.

Richard Spencer and Aleksandr Dugin, scary as they
are, are not unique cases. They are part of a new Fascist
International that is becoming more and more assertive.
As incredible as it may seem, the alt-right even managed
to establish a beachhead in the Trump White House.[11] In
the chapter of Allan Bloom's *The Closing of the American*

Mind entitled "The Nietzscheanization of the Left or Vice Versa," Bloom wrote the following: "Nietzsche's colossal political failure is attested to by the facts that the Right, which was his only hope that his teaching would have its proper effect, has utterly disappeared, and he himself was tainted in its ugly last gasp, while today virtually every Nietzschean, as well as Heideggerian, is a leftist."[12] I'm not sure whether that sentence was ever fully true, but it's certainly not true today.

Bloom's most ambitious successor in the claim that the left has been hoodwinked by Nietzsche is himself a man of the left—namely, Geoff Waite. But Waite goes beyond Bloom in further claiming that this was a deliberate project of Nietzsche's: "Nietzsche programmed his reception in unconscious, subliminal ways."[13] This is, as Waite knows, a difficult thesis to prove, but I think it would be naïve to dismiss it too quickly, and I think it's a shame that intellectuals of the left (or just intellectuals in general) haven't been more appreciative of Waite's sharp insights into what he calls "Nietzsche's *intent* to have an influenza-like impact on the future."[14] As Waite writes, "Left-Nietzscheans and Right-Nietzscheans find themselves in the same bed together, as day breaks and the Dionysian revel of the night is transformed into hangover, and no owl of Athena has taken flight."[15] If, as Waite also suggests, Nietzsche has become (or has manipulated his way into becoming) the master thinker of "the real Right and fake Left alike,"[16] then a very profound engagement with Nietzsche is required. And as Waite again fully understands, the same level of engagement needs to be applied to Heidegger as well.

For decades, young intellectuals have been encouraged by their teachers to regard Nietzsche and Heidegger (the two Pied Pipers of contemporary culture and philosophy?) as friends and allies of the contemporary left—though there have been isolated voices within the intellectual community warning that perhaps there is a little more poison in these thinkers than their enthusiasts in the academy have bargained for. And it may well be that we are currently seeing the coming-to-fruition of some of this poison. One notable case in point is the Nietzschean doctrine claiming that appeals to truth are largely ideological, designed to obfuscate the deeper realities of power and resentment. This doctrine was enthusiastically taken up by Michel Foucault with his attempt to see truth as a normative aspiration exposed as a mask for what are in reality cynical "regimes of truth."[17] And what do we have today? "Post-truth"! (As Timothy Snyder rightly and importantly points out, "Post-truth is prefascism."[18]) Nietzschean notions, mediated by supposedly emancipatory appropriations of Nietzsche, seem to have left us vulnerable to harsh new ideologies that appear to regard respect for truth as a snare for the strong set by the weak (as Nietzsche largely presents it).

***

Let's sketch the essential historical/philosophical background. The French Revolution represented the key moment of fundamental sea change in European consciousness and politics. To put it very crudely and simply, prior to 1789, one had a political world oriented fundamentally toward hierarchy; after 1789, one had a political world fundamentally oriented toward equality and the free judgments of individuals who determine for themselves what their lives are about rather than having it dictated from above. That's an enormous change in the ordering of human society and the shape of moral consciousness! It's not an accident that the most virulent enemies of modern liberalism and modern democracy—such as Joseph de Maistre in the early nineteenth century and Nietzsche in the late nineteenth century—directed their most intense polemical energies against the French Revolution.[19] If one subscribes to hard-line reactionary politics, as both Maistre and Nietzsche do in their very different ways, then the French Revolution will present itself as the moment when European civilization begins to slide into the abyss. That's the decisive turning point. A view of society where all individuals are fundamentally equal or a view of society where people can live meaningful lives only under the banner of fundamental hierarchy: this is an either/or, not a moral-political choice that can be submitted to compromise or splitting the difference.

Nietzsche rightly zeroed in on the French Revolution as the linchpin because it poses the essential issue: one either sees egalitarianism as essential to the proper acknowledgment of universal human dignity, or one sees it as the destruction of what's most human because it's incompatible with human nobility rightly understood. Let me cite another key nineteenth-century theorist, Alexis de Tocqueville, whose central message in *Democracy in America* could be paraphrased as follows: even aristocrats like me must resign ourselves to the fact that we live in a new post–French Revolution world, a world primordially defined by democratic ideals. Much will be lost,

Tocqueville makes clear, in the transition from a world of social hierarchy to a world of social equality, but whatever those human losses may add up to, the democratic world must be embraced on account of its superior justice.[20] The political reactionaries I've mentioned were never willing to concede that point, and as a question of political philosophy, the debate between liberals like Tocqueville and antiliberals like Nietzsche is still in progress (and probably always will be).

Having referred to Maistre and Nietzsche as the "rejectionist front" vis-à-vis the Enlightenment, let me also mention that a more complete version of the story here would have to commence with the Protestant Reformation. The German poet Heinrich Heine wrote that "the philosophical revolution [unfolded in European modernity] . . . emerged from the religious one, and [this revolution in philosophy,] indeed, is nothing other than the logical conclusion of Protestantism."[21] Heine's suggestion, in my view, captures something essential in how one should understand the intellectual history of modernity. Arguably, the key development was the Reformation's insistence that lay readers judge scripture for themselves, via vernacular editions of the Bible, unmediated by reliance on clerical elites with privileged access to sacred languages. One had to cultivate in ordinary people the confidence that judgment regarding the ultimate questions of human existence could repose on their own responsibility rather than being appropriated by supposed spiritual elites. This was in itself an intellectual revolution of inestimable proportions, and (as Heine's thesis implies) any subsequent liberation of ordinary lay judgment was founded on the enormous democratizing promise contained in the Reformation. It is no surprise, then, that both Maistre and Nietzsche reject the Reformation as bitterly as they do, for it is what ultimately clears the way for what became the Enlightenment and then liberalism.[22]

Highly relevant to the contemporary neofascist revival is the fact that since the Enlightenment, a line of important thinkers has considered life in liberal modernity to be profoundly dehumanizing. Thinkers in this category include, but are not limited to, Maistre, Nietzsche, Carl Schmitt, and Heidegger. For such thinkers, liberal modernity is *so* humanly degrading that one ought to (if one could) undo the French Revolution and its egalitarian ideal and perhaps cancel out the whole moral legacy of Christianity. For all of them, hierarchy and rootedness are more morally compelling than equality and individual liberty; democracy diminishes our humanity rather than elevates it. We are unlikely to understand why fascism is still kicking around in the twenty-first century unless we are able to grasp why certain intellectuals of the early twentieth century gravitated toward fascism—namely, on account of a grim preoccupation with the perceived soullessness of modernity and a resolve to embrace *any* politics, however extreme, that seemed to them to promise "spiritual renewal," to quote Heidegger.[23]

For these thinkers (and their contemporary adherents), liberalism, egalitarianism, and democracy are a recipe for absolute deracination and hence for a profound contraction of the human spirit, which presumably is what Heidegger had in mind when he spoke of spiritual renewal. In one decisive text, Heidegger asserted that he learned from Nietzsche that democracy is ultimately nihilism. We can unpack that seemingly odd statement by saying that for the political-philosophical tradition within which Heidegger stands, the French Revolution inaugurates a moral universe where authority resides with the herd, not with the shepherd; with the mass, not with the elite; and as a consequence, ultimately the whole experience of life spirals down into unbearable shallowness and meaninglessness. That's a short unpacking; the full story will be the work of this book as a whole. What's true of philosophy in general applies especially to these thinkers: in order to see what is at stake in their thought, one has to look at the forest, not just the trees. (I'm inclined to view the interpretation of great thinkers as something akin to the vocation of murder detectives solving particularly difficult cases. It is, I would say, forensic riddle-solving without the blood.)

***

Let us come back once more to Richard Spencer. Prior to the election of Trump, it would have been unthinkable to imagine that a lunatic ideologue like him could have any connections, however remote, to the corridors of power in the most powerful republic in the Western world. It is a sobering reflection on our current situation to note that that is no longer true. Soon after the election, Spencer, obviously energized by an outcome that he (and many others) saw as a triumph for the alt-right, released a podcast in which he said the following: "I think [ex-White House Chief Strategist Stephen K.] Bannon is a wild card, and a wild card is good. . . . Bannon has made gestures towards us; he's said Breitbart is a platform for the alt-right. He's apparently read Julius Evola and Alexander Dugin. Make of that what you will. . . . We want a wild card; we want change. So, I think Bannon is a good thing."[24] Bannon himself played to this kind of radicalism when he boasted that the Trump regime, under his guidance, would entail "the birth of a new political order."

Where do we look in trying to trace the source of the virulently antiliberal, antidemocratic radicalism of a Richard Spencer? According to an August 31, 2015, story in the *Chicago Tribune*, Spencer "credits his time at the University of Chicago . . . for his intellectual flowering, which includes a kinship with the philosophy of Friedrich Nietzsche."[25] During a master's program, completed in 2003, he apparently took a graduate seminar on Nietzsche and was hooked. Obviously, not many people taking seminars on the thought of Nietzsche in grad school will turn into neofascists. It doesn't follow from that fact that there aren't things in Nietzsche's work (or in Heidegger's) *capable* of turning people into neofascists.[26] And clearly this wouldn't be the urgent cause for worry that it currently is if it weren't true that our contemporary world is populated by far more neofascists than we may have imagined until quite recently.[27]

One of the typically odious far-right websites features a book review of a recent book by Jason Jorjani in which the reviewer suggests that "Nietzsche, Heidegger, Schmitt, [Alain] de Benoist, [Guillaume] Faye, Dugin, etc." constitute "the alt-Right canon." The omission of Evola is surprising, but the listing of Nietzsche, Heidegger, and Schmitt as 1, 2, 3 is surely quite telling. Richard Spencer, at a press conference during the same alt-right gathering at which he delivered his "Hail Trump" speech, said that the difference between the alt-right and others on the right is that "we actually read books." And these are the books that they read. Obviously, we don't want this to turn into an exercise in conspiracy theorizing. Let's leave that to the ideologues. But if something is dangerous, we need to be aware that it's dangerous. And that awareness has been woefully lacking in regard to several of the most influential philosophers of the last 150 years. The contemporary resurgence of far-right politics forces us to command heightened vigilance with respect to the directly practical implications of what Mark Lilla in 2001 called "the reckless mind," or what Georg Lukács in 1952 called "the destruction of reason."

"Where are the barbarians of the twentieth century?" Nietzsche poses that question in *The Will to Power* (§ 868). Those sympathetic to Nietzsche (apart from fascists) have needed to find some way to brush past it and many similar statements, treating them as a kind of joke or just a provocation. Of course merely a few decades after Nietzsche wrote these words, the world knew exactly where these barbarians could be found—in the very heart of Europe. We could perhaps revert to the benign view of why Nietzsche asked that question if someone could give us absolute assurances that there would be no similar barbarians in the twenty-first century. But today we know for a fact that no such assurances are forthcoming.

Clover, in *Black Wind, White Snow*, writes the following about the ideological landscape in Russia during the Yeltsin years: "For many provincial Russian youths, languishing in stultifying mining towns and crushing poverty, the NBP [the neofascist political party co-led by Dugin and Eduard Limonov in the 1990s] offered a rush of adrenaline."[28] It seems strange to think that there could be anything in common between Yeltsin-era Russia and contemporary America; yet ideologically, surveying the scene in 2017, it does seem as if there is some kind of thread joining them. Let me try out my own version of Clover's sentence (which may be a highly imperfect parallel in all kinds of ways and yet may still capture something important): "For many young people in the suburbs and small towns of the American heartland, facing the despair of unemployment or the even worse despair of stultifying and meaningless work in anonymous offices, the alt-right offers a rush of adrenaline."

Hopefully no reader of my book will draw from it the unfortunate conclusion that we should just walk away from Nietzsche and Heidegger—that is, stop reading them. On the contrary, I think we need to read them in ways that make us more conscious of, more reflective about, and more self-critical of the *limits* of the liberal view of life and hence what defines that view of life. That's something that we should certainly do, and if we fail to do it, it will be at our own peril. But if one is handling intellectually radioactive materials, one has to be much less naïve about what one is dealing with. We must read these thinkers with our eyes fully open to the aspects of their thought that express revulsion for and a despising of the liberal (and liberal-democratic) view of life, for those aspects of their thought are unquestionably a part—indeed, a central part—of their thought. We need to open our eyes, at once *intellectually*, *morally*, and *politically*, to just how dangerous they are.

Reading Nietzsche in an Age of Resurgent Fascism

The sort of unqualified and utterly unsuitable people who may one day come to invoke my authority is a thought that fills me with dread.

—Friedrich Nietzsche

As is well known, the intellectual left has found much to its liking in the philosophies of ultraright thinkers such as Nietzsche, Heidegger, and Carl Schmitt.[1] Why this is so is hardly obvious, and one cannot help wondering about where one should look for the full story on this curious feature of intellectual life in recent decades. Whether this is something that has an intraintellectual explanation or whether it has a kind of "sociology of knowledge" explanation is not something I will attempt to pursue here. I'm only saying it merits further reflection. But what I *will* pursue in the following discussion (and I will do something similar in the next chapter) is a reexamination of one of these thinkers whom many of us have read and been excited by in our youth, asking whether we can any longer afford to read him while filtering out the ultra-right dimensions of his thought. It's all too easy to read Nietzsche, appreciating the stuff one likes while taking with a grain of salt all the unpleasant stuff that doesn't suit contemporary tastes. But if the far right is making a come-back today (which I believe it is), then this starts to look like an intolerable intellectual luxury.

***

I first started reading Nietzsche around 1973. By some unaccountable Nietzsche-style fatality, I stumbled on a copy of *Thus Spoke Zarathustra* in the stacks at McGill University. I was an enthusiast right from the start. (What better antidote to growing up amid the banality and conformism of suburban life in North America?) Occasionally, one would come across critics highlighting the protofascist dimensions of Nietzsche's thought.[2] There may be scary lines scattered throughout his works. But on the whole, Nietzsche seemed to present himself as—to borrow Tracy Strong's phrase—"a voice for liberation."[3]

There is a repellent though famous photograph (by Heinrich Hoffmann) that we contemporary readers of Nietzsche must confront. It features Hitler in 1934 at the Nietzsche Archives in Weimar.[4] No one who respects the mind or literary genius of Nietzsche will find it easy to look at that horrible image. But we have to be resolute in asking ourselves, Why was Hitler motivated to stage the taking of that photograph? It was a deliberate act of state-craft,[5] and whether or not Nietzsche would have welcomed being enlisted in those ideological purposes (it is a virtual certainty that it would have caused him significant pain), he was nonetheless complicit in the Hitlerite appropriation of his legacy because there were things in his oeuvre that invited that appropriation and that made it attractive for Hitler to lay claim to him just as Lenin and Stalin had laid claim to Marx. And take note: the Nazi appropriation of Nietzsche didn't end with Hitler. Nicholas Goodrick-Clarke, an authority on Aryan cults and "esoteric Nazism," writes that "*The Anti-Christ*, Nietzsche's trenchant rejection of Christianity written in 1888, is now current as an anti-Christian manifesto among white power activists in America and Europe."[6]

Similarly, we need to think hardheadedly and concretely about exactly what Nietzsche may have intended when he spoke, both in *Beyond Good and Evil* (§ 208) and in *Ecce Homo* ("Why I Am a Destiny," § 1), about the coming age of *große Politik* and about himself as the prophet of *große Politik*.[7] Apart from emphasizing its Pan-European character and its not being limited to petty-nationalistic horizons, Nietzsche never really elaborated what this kind of politics would look like in concrete terms. Clearly, the implication was that it was a kind of imperial political project, gesturing back to glory-oriented empires of the past.[8] In other words, this was a blank check, and a distinctly dangerous one, given the projects of the politics of empire that were (as he predicted) to appear on the scene a few short decades later. When Nietzsche, in *Twilight of the Idols* ("Skirmishes of an Untimely Man," § 39), affirms the need for cultural norms that are "anti-liberal to the point of malice," he means exactly what he says. When Nietzsche wrote in § 251 of *Beyond Good and Evil* that what defines the European problem as he understands it ("what is *serious* for me") is "the cultivation of a new caste to rule over Europe," he really meant "caste" (*Kaste*), he really meant "rule" (*regierenden*), and he really meant "Europe." These were not metaphors for something "spiritual." This is politically innocent only on the assumption that Nietzsche would never be read by people who took him at his word. We surely know by now that this assumption is untenable.

Hans-Georg Gadamer once wrote, "I am in favor of a government and politics that would allow for mutual understanding and the freedom of all. . . . [This] has been self-evident to any European since the French Revolution, since Hegel and Kant."[9] This statement is in fact quite false (and Gadamer should have known that it was false). The reality is that there has been in Europe a long succession of radical thinkers who rejected the liberal egalitarianism of the French Revolution root and branch. (Gadamer ought to have known this because his own philosophical mentor, Martin Heidegger, was one of these radical thinkers and also because he lived for twelve horrendous years under a regime that expressed the same ideological rejection.[10]) Almost certainly the most important of these philosophers associated with the tradition of resolute repudiation of liberal modernity in all its moral, political, and cultural dimensions is Friedrich Nietzsche. Generations of readers of Nietzsche have never failed to find ways to "launder" or "sanitize" or at least take the edge off his hatred of freedom and equality as interpreted by modernity. Reading Nietzsche as benign or even as emancipatory would be tolerable if we could be assured that we wouldn't face a second attempt at putting Nietzschean extremism into practice with extremely malevolent consequences for the world. But the recent and unexpected rise of the populist far right tells us, on the contrary, that we must fear and be vigilant about (to quote Conor Cruise O'Brien again) "what his messages might effect when they reached minds which were as bold in action as he was bold in thought."

Julius Evola's Nietzsche

I am no man, I am dynamite.

—Friedrich Nietzsche[11]

When a representative of the twentieth-century European far right such as Julius Evola reads Nietzsche, what does he absorb as the pertinent political-cultural message? In the very first reference to Nietzsche in *Ride the Tiger*, Evola cites him as "a great precursor."[12] Nietzsche was right that what was promised by bourgeois civilization is a complete fraud: it delivers "a soulless, mechanistic, and purely earthly civilization" that is in its "terminal state."[13] The civilizational ends privileged by liberalism and democracy are brought to fruition by socialism—namely, an era of the last man accurately depicted by Nietzsche: "a human integrity traded for that which might suit socialized cattle."[14] In common with Nietzsche, Evola's view is that the making available of "a plentiful, easy, and comfortable existence" (the ideal of life shared between Marxism and Western liberalism) counts for nothing: "Hegel rightly wrote that the epochs of material well-being are blank pages in the history book."[15] "True leaders do not exist today" because, as Nietzsche rightly perceived, the supposed ruling class is in fact dedicated to "the virtues of the serfs."[16] The core problem is that living in a world governed by "the regime of the masses" (the regime of "the mediocre soul"), where one ought to have hierarchies of "rank and spiritual superiority," one instead has merely hierarchies defined by technical expertise.[17] This, for Evola, constitutes "the absurdity of modern existence,"[18] although exactly how fascism is meant to supply an antidote to this absurdity remains a mystery. "The general situation characterized by Nietzsche remains: 'The struggle for supremacy amidst conditions that are worth nothing: this civilization of great cities, newspapers, fever, uselessness.'"[19] Knowing oneself to be inhabiting a civilization that is worthless, the Nietzschean aristocrat in a society of slaves "feels himself belonging to a different humanity and recognizes the desert around himself."[20] To be sure, Evola regards Nietzsche's vitalism as a "pseudo-solution" and suggests that Nietzsche's failure to move from immanence to transcendence "generates a higher voltage than the circuit can sustain," quoting an 1881 letter from Nietzsche to Peter Gast in which Nietzsche describes himself as "one of those machines that might explode."[21] In any case, the post-1789 world is collapsing precipitously, and insofar as one can contribute to speeding up rather than postponing its demise, anything that might "prop it up and prolong its existence artificially" should be avoided.[22]

We know that Nietzsche longed for "barbarians of the twentieth century." Would he have hoped to inspire, for instance, far-right terrorists in the 1970s? Perhaps not. But we know that Nietzsche's votary, Julius Evola, was perfectly happy performing the role of a guru for terrorists: "Young postwar neo-fascists sat at Evola's feet to hear this oracle of aristocratic values and war with modernity." Inspired by Evola's "philosophy of total war," these disciples of Nietzsche's disciple "unleashed a surge of black terrorism in Italy."[23] The thought by which Nietzsche was "filled with dread" (namely, vulgar Nietzscheanism) was not an idle one.

The Challenge of Nietzsche

How do we respond, humanly speaking, to a thinker who simply doesn't believe in human dignity or the equal rights of all human beings? Who self-consciously denounces the whole moral universe conjured up by the French Revolution and believes that it didn't secure a higher status for humanity but on the contrary incalculably diminished our stature? Who believes that in order to redeem such a thing as human dignity, we need to strive for something *far beyond* our current humanity, and in order to do *that*, need to restore the conceptions of radical hierarchy that were banished by the French Revolution and the whole post–French Revolution moral universe? We would barely know what to make of such a creature—we wouldn't really be able to comprehend him even if he were staring us in the face! Stranger still, imagine that such a thinker went on to become one of the most influential thinkers of the twentieth century and was championed to a very large extent by intellectuals of the left! Bizarre! Yet I am not sketching some hypothetical philosopher on Mars; this is Friedrich Nietzsche, who has influenced and shaped contemporary culture and intellectual life to a staggering degree. What do we make of all this?

Chapter 1

A key aspect of Nietzsche's appeal (as a *rhetorician*, one might say, rather than as a thinker per se) is how generative he is, both with respect to new styles and with respect to provocative content, how protean he is—the sheer abundance in his writing and in his intellectual activity. There's something for everyone! Something for every taste, as it were. There's Nietzsche, the philosopher who demolishes the whole history of metaphysics. There's Nietzsche, the ruthless debunker of religion and moralism. There's Nietzsche, the affirmer of the body, severely challenging the privileging of mind or spirit going back to Plato. There's Nietzsche, the prophet of the collapse of the cultural hollowness of modernity. And so on. There's a radical pluralism in Nietzsche's mode of thought that completely outflanks or trumps any preceding mode of intellectual pluralism.

On the other hand, let us recall the memorable dictum from Martin Heidegger's lectures on Nietzsche: "Each thinker thinks only one *single* thought."[24] That's what makes them great thinkers. I truly believe that Heidegger was right about that. (If we were to follow Isaiah Berlin's advice to orient theory toward pluralistic foxes rather than monistic hedgehogs, we would ultimately be left with no theory canon at all.) And if it's true, it must be true of Nietzsche as well (especially since Heidegger formulated his principle with Nietzsche specifically in mind). So we must ask, What is the *singular* philosophical impulse in Nietzsche amid what looks like unbounded pluralism? Yet searching for a "true" Nietzsche or an "essential" Nietzsche (which I think we must do) looks as if it can't possibly be squared with Nietzsche's own emphasis on resisting singular truths or singular essences. I will treat Nietzsche's pluralism as a rhetoric (a highly effective rhetoric!) and attempt to spell out one possible reading of the "essence" of Nietzsche's intellectual concerns. What I'll suggest is that all of Nietzsche's literary virtuosity—which is undeniable, which seduces its readers and was *intended* to seduce them—is in the service of this essential core commitment.

Consider a passage on Nietzsche penned by Thomas Mann that I basically endorse:

> Much as his largely aphoristic work glitters in a thousand colored facets, many as are the surface contradictions that can be demonstrated in his books—he was from the start a coherent whole, remained always the same. In the writings of the youthful professor— the *Thoughts Out of Season*, *The Birth of Tragedy*, and the 1873 treatise *The Philosopher*—are to be found more than the seeds of his later dogmas, the tidings he was to hurl down from his mountaintop. More than seeds because these dogmas—which in his opinion were *glad* tidings—were already contained in perfect and finished form in those works. What changed was solely the accentuation, the pitch, the gestures. These grew steadily more frantic, shriller, more grotesque and terrible. . . . [W]e cannot sufficiently stress the complete unity and coherence of Nietzsche's life works.[25]

Geoff Waite quotes a letter from Nietzsche to Paul Deussen dated January 3, 1888, in which Nietzsche acknowledges that there is a "center" to his thought, a "great passion in the service of which I live."[26] That may seem like stating the obvious—how could Nietzsche have sustained his gargantuan literary output if that weren't the case?—yet there are legions of Nietzsche's readers who refuse to believe it. Waite's view, for which I have much sympathy, is that this unspecified center is esoteric and that much of what Nietzsche's readers have always associated with him is merely exoteric rhetoric intended to seduce, dupe, and ultimately hijack those readers. Let me share my own proposal with respect to what this one central, animating Nietzschean idea might be: Western civilization is going down the toilet because of too much emphasis on truth and rationality and too much emphasis on equal human dignity.

***

The initial thought on which my presentation of Nietzsche is founded is that Nietzsche's positive philosophy is all nonsense or lunacy: *Übermenschen*, will to power, eternal recurrence of the same, a return to ancien régime–type European aristocracy. It's impossible to take any of that seriously. Those wild ideas are simply the expression of a desperation on Nietzsche's part in needing "solutions." Also, I think that one always has to keep in mind that one can't conjure up the notion of *Übermenschen* without simultaneously conjuring up the notion of *Untermenschen* (superhuman and subhuman, respectively). I don't think Nietzsche himself ever shied away from embracing that significant (and horrifying) entailment of the idea of the *Übermensch*,[27] and it goes without saying that the Nazis, forty years later, didn't fail to draw the same entailment.

But the cultural diagnosis that animates Nietzsche's work is *not* nonsense. That cultural diagnosis is what Nietzsche's imaginary mirage-like "solutions" are meant to be solutions *for*. (The same goes for Heidegger.) So we can put to one side all the phantom solutions and put all our focus on the critical diagnosis: what Nietzsche considers the comprehensive malady of a sick civilization. That's what I hope to do in what follows, picking up instructive clues in two short, early works of his and then tracing similar themes in more mature works. That will conduct us, I hope, into the essence of what drives him as a thinker and has made him so seductive for those who read him (including many of the towering thinkers of the early twentieth century).

I want to zero in on two key notions that I think define what's most important in Nietzsche as a political philosopher. The first is the idea of the "horizonlessness" of modernity. That's a mouthful, to be sure, but it's just about pronounceable. In Nietzsche's view, to live a meaningful life, one needs to have a real sense of vibrancy and vitality with respect to who one takes oneself to be and what one considers oneself to be living *for*. That is, one needs a *life-affirming* experience of existence. Life, to be life, needs to affirm itself and push itself to transcend itself, and none of that is possible without a culture with definite boundaries that understands with utter clarity what its purpose is—its "whither and wherefor." Life without this life-affirming sense isn't real life. Coasting through life, not knowing what one is living for, is a phantom life or a hollow life, a life without substance. And *cultures*, as legislated by individuals with the genius to do this, are essential in determining whether one inhabits a life-affirming (real) existence or a life-negating (shadow) existence. But these cultures are *ceasing to exist!* Nietzsche is emphatic on the dual theme of the indispensability of these cultures and their loss or eclipse. Hence the tone of real desperation that runs through all of Nietzsche's writing. We have to fix this, and fix it very soon, or our human experience will shrink to utter pointlessness, which is what the famous depiction of the "last men" is meant to dramatize. "Modern" cultures aren't real cultures—they are *pseudo*cultures.[28] Moderns are becoming too reflective about their membership in these cultures and about the equal validity of alternative cultures for life-affirming cultures to be sustainable much longer (insofar as they still exist at all). The history of modernity is the history of the disappearance of the kind of cultures required in order for life to be life-affirming.

Related to this is the fact that there are important texts where Nietzsche expresses hostility to modern secularity and expresses receptivity to the great historical world religions. This, notwithstanding the fact that Nietzsche is—not without reason!—customarily regarded as in effect *one of the founding atheists of late modernity.* This seems paradoxical—and it *is* paradoxical! But there's an intelligible logic here: civilization-defining religions legislate robust cultural horizons. Modernity, including (perhaps especially) *secular* modernity, *opens* these horizons, which in Nietzsche's view defeats all possibility of a life-affirming existence.[29] Again, that seems highly paradoxical; in my view it is *the* defining paradox of Nietzsche. Nietzsche *hates* Christianity—especially Protestant Christianity. But he doesn't hate certain aspects of ancient Hebraic culture, or ancient Hinduism, or Islam, or ancient paganism; *quite the contrary.* The fact that Christianity, and again especially Protestant Christianity, has served as an indispensable condition of modernity—assuming that's true—*counts against Christianity!* In the Preface to *Beyond Good and Evil,* Nietzsche refers disdainfully to the newspaper-reading Enlightenment. Why would someone who rejects the whole of Western theism as a lie refer to the Enlightenment in this kind of disdainful way? If we can't answer *that* question, then—I would suggest—we have no possibility of access to Nietzsche's distinctive theoretical stance. There *is* a logic here, however paradoxical—namely, Nietzsche as a heroic or epic religion-loving atheist![30]

The second idea that I want to privilege is the notion that a tragic experience of life and the universe, or even the possibility of that in any meaningful sense, is being drained away by the whole trajectory of our civilization in its totality. Nietzsche believes in cultures that are life-affirming, and Nietzsche believes that the most impressive human culture is a "tragic" culture (a culture committed to a "pessimism of strength," as he notably puts it). This shapes his stance toward Christianity and toward everything that he thinks flows culturally from Christianity. For Nietzsche, *repudiation of Christianity constitutes the necessary condition of a return to an aristocracy-centered culture.* What Tocqueville *worries about* with respect to living in a pervasively democratic/egalitarian civilization is ramped up by Nietzsche into pure rhetorical *hysteria.* The idea, one assumes, is that rhetoric of that kind is needed to convince people that the crisis of European culture really is a crisis. These two notions—the idea of horizonlessness and the idea of replacing a banal, Christianity-shaped culture with a tragic and therefore noble culture—are obviously related in some way, which it remains for us to trace if we can. And we also want to trace the effects of these notions in the thinking of Nietzsche's three most important intellectual heirs: Sigmund Freud, Max Weber, and Martin Heidegger. But before we begin doing that, let's survey some notable texts in Nietzsche that give expression to the first of these two (in my view) master themes.

Salient Texts

Naturally, what image one has of Nietzsche will be a function of which texts one privileges. This relates to the point I've already made about the almost insane fecundity or overabundance of Nietzsche's texts, themes, and cultural or philosophical gestures. And of course I have my own favorite texts. In this section, I'll quote from some of these favorites in order to sketch what I take to be the Nietzschean core. Let me add, if it needs to be added, that these are "favorite texts" not in the sense that they necessarily articulate a philosophically attractive view but simply in the sense that they capture what I see as the "essence" of Nietzsche.

Nietzsche is commonly approached as a philosopher of perspectivalism, playfulness, creativity, the subverting of metaphysical dogmas, openness to new vistas, and so on. Read in that way, Nietzsche can come across as an *extension* of the modern Enlightenment, as a kind of *radicalized liberalism* (John Stuart Mill on steroids!). Unquestionably, all of that is an important aspect of his rhetoric. But it certainly doesn't tell the whole story. My chosen texts will play up the opposing side—Nietzsche as a thinker who worries about excessive openness and the exploding of fixed horizons—and hence will challenge quite squarely those familiar images of Nietzsche. My first four texts are drawn from two books by early Nietzsche and two books by mature Nietzsche to try to suggest that my counterimage of Nietzsche runs throughout his work: a trajectory stretching from start to finish, so to speak. What matters was there from the start (as Thomas Mann was entirely right to point out).

1. In his important early text, *On the Uses and Disadvantages of History for Life*, Nietzsche argues that life, in order for vibrant agency to be meaningful or simply in order for life to be life, requires firm and definite bounded horizons, of which late modernity, on account of its privileging of knowledge over action, is incapable. This theme runs through much of the work, but here is one sample of the many that could be quoted:

> A man's historical sense and knowledge can be very limited, his horizon as narrow as that of a dweller in the Alps, all his judgments may involve injustice and he may falsely suppose that all his experiences are original to him—yet in spite of this injustice and error he will nonetheless stand there in superlative health and vigour, a joy to all who see him; while close beside him a man far more just and instructed than he sickens and collapses because the lines of his horizon are always restlessly changing, because he can no longer extricate himself from the delicate net of his judiciousness and truth for a simple act of will and desire.[31]

Nietzsche was interested in how, for a very few rare individuals, the debunking of morality and universal reason could liberate them to refashion their selves with much greater freedom and creativity. But Nietzsche also believed that the vast majority of the inhabitants of modernity were sunken far too deeply in mediocrity for this project of self-creation to be of any relevance to them. Contrary to what is suggested by countless left-Nietzscheans, Nietzsche, of course, *wasn't* interested in promoting greater openness, tolerance, or inclusion for the marginalized. His beef against modern post-Christian civilization was not that it was illiberal and insufficiently inclusive but rather that it was too egalitarian and too weak in legislating definite horizons within which the mediocre majority could find a clear purpose in life. That's why Nietzsche wanted to encourage greater strength and robustness of will for the few capable of refashioning themselves: having exercised the will necessary to recreate their own selves, they could also legislate new norms that would put an end to the insipid and irresolute cultural vacuum into which the post-Christian egalitarian culture had collapsed. In Nietzsche's view, the "spiritlessness" of modernity flows from modernity's excess of knowledge or excess of preoccupation with truth.[32]

2. The theme of the dissolution of stable anchors of cultural experience also figures prominently in the next of Nietzsche's four *Untimely Mediations*—namely, *Schopenhauer as Educator*:

> When [the genuine philosopher] thinks of the haste and hurry now universal, of the increasing velocity of life, of the cessation of all contemplativeness and simplicity, he almost thinks that what he is seeing are the symptoms of a total extermination and uprooting of culture. The waters of religion are ebbing away and

leaving behind swamps or stagnant pools; the nations are again drawing away from one another in the most hostile fashion and long to tear one another to pieces. The sciences, pursued without any restraint and in a spirit of the blindest *laissez faire*, are shattering and dissolving all firmly held belief; the educated classes and states are being swept along by a hugely contemptible money economy. The world has never been more worldly, never poorer in love and goodness. The educated classes are no longer lighthouses or refuges in the midst of this turmoil of secularization; they themselves grow daily more restless, thoughtless, and loveless. Everything, contemporary art and science included, serves the coming barbarism.[33]

Lukács quotes a passage from early Nietzsche that provides crucial elucidation of what Nietzsche had in mind in criticizing "secularization" in this *Schopenhauer as Educator* text: "The drive . . . to disseminate culture as widely as possible has its origins in a total secularization, by which culture is reduced to a means of gain and of earthly happiness in the vulgar sense."[34] It wouldn't be wide of the mark to say that Nietzsche's later idea of "the last man" was another way of articulating what he meant by "secularization" in these early texts. As Lukács highlights quite well, it basically means that the universalization of culture as conceived by liberal modernity entails the reduction of culture in its sacredness or holiness to what is utterly profane. For late Nietzsche as for early Nietzsche, there is no worse disaster for humanity.

3. Let's now skip ahead to two late texts. First, *Beyond Good and Evil*, § 188:

Chapter 1

What is essential "in heaven and on earth" seems to be, to say it once more, that there should be *obedience* over a long period of time and in a *single* direction: given that, something always develops, and has developed, for whose sake it is worthwhile to live on earth; for example, virtue, art, music, dance, reason, spirituality—something transfiguring, subtle, mad, and divine. The long unfreedom of the spirit, the mistrustful constraint in the communicability of thoughts, the discipline thinkers imposed on themselves to think within the directions laid down by a church or court . . . all this, however forced, capricious, hard, gruesome, and anti-rational, has shown itself to be the means through which the European spirit has been trained to strength, ruthless curiosity, and subtle mobility, though admittedly in the process an irreplaceable amount of strength and spirit had to be crushed, stifled, and ruined.[35]

Nietzsche's cardinal idea here is encapsulated best in *The Will to Power*, § 961, where he celebrates "protracted *despotic moralities*" because "they tense the bow" (a persistent and defining metaphor for Nietzsche, also to be found in *Genealogy of Morals*, first essay, § 12, and the preface as well as §§ 206 and 262 of *Beyond Good and Evil*). The idea is for human cultures to shoot consummately high, and indulgent modernity, with its flabby, liberal norms, doesn't stretch the bow with nearly enough tension to be able to do that; hence its decisive inferiority to premodern "despotic moralities." One could say that the intended purpose of the Enlightenment and of modern liberalism is to undo the "crushing, stifling, and ruining" of the human mind and spirit that Nietzsche refers to in the text we have quoted from *Beyond Good and Evil*, § 188, but at a price that Nietzsche regards as absolutely unacceptable.

4. Our fourth (closely related) text is *Twilight of the Idols*, "Skirmishes of an Untimely Man," § 39:

> *Critique of modernity.* Our institutions are no good any more: on that there is universal agreement. However, it is not their fault but ours. Once we have lost all the instincts out of which institutions grow, we lose institutions altogether because we are no longer good for them. . . . Witness *modern marriage*. All rationality has clearly vanished from modern marriage; yet that is no objection to marriage, but to modernity. The rationality of marriage—that lay in the husband's sole juridical responsibility, which gave marriage a center of gravity, while today it limps on both legs. The rationality of marriage—that lay in its indissolubility in principle, which lent it an accent that could be heard above the accident of feeling, passion, and what is merely momentary. It also lay in the family's responsibility for the choice of a spouse. . . . Marriage as an institution involves the affirmation of the largest and most enduring form of organization: when society cannot affirm itself as a whole, down to the most distant generations, then marriage has altogether no meaning. Modern marriage has lost its meaning—consequently one abolishes it.[36]

This guy is not a liberal! Georg Simmel has expressed the essential point extremely well: "There is no more severe judge of everything anarchic, undisciplined, and soft than Nietzsche, who finds the reason for the engulfing contemporary decadence in the disappearance of strict discipline, piety, and authority in the face of the ignoble tendency toward equalization and universal happiness."[37] The appeal to "piety" may appear jarring in relation to conventional readings of Nietzsche, but I think that Simmel gets this right.

If one reads Nietzsche mediated through Michel Foucault, one is likely to read him as offering *a radicalized version of liberalism*—what I once called Foucault's "hyper-liberalism."[38] Plenty of theorists today read him that way, influenced by Foucault or by other French left-Nietzscheans. Nietzsche himself would be horrified. This should be too obvious to need saying, but today it probably does need saying: Nietzsche is not Foucault! Not only is he a cultural arch-reactionary; he regards old-fashioned nineteenth-century liberalism—to say nothing of radicalized twentieth- and twenty-first-century versions—as rendering culture per se impossible. That's why he presents modernity as a form of barbarism. (That's Heidegger's view as well, notwithstanding the fact that French left-Nietzscheans have embraced Heidegger no less than they have embraced Nietzsche!)

5. There's a fifth text that I'd like to bring in in this context: the famous "parable of the madman" in *Gay Science* (§ 125). There's one particular aspect of the text that's worth underscoring in relation to the texts I've already quoted. After the madman informs his listeners in the marketplace that he and they are the murderers of God, he asks the following questions: "How could we drink up the sea? *Who gave us the sponge to wipe away the entire horizon?* [My italics.] What were we doing

when we unchained this earth from its sun? Whither is it moving now? Whither are we moving? Away from all suns? Are we not plunging continually? Backward, sideward, forward, in all directions? Is there still any up or down? Do we not feel the breath of empty space?" Again the idea of horizonlessness! The entire horizon has been wiped away. And with no horizon, we have no means of orientation—no up or down, no left or right. All we have is empty space, through which we float without any sense of what direction might be the right one. All authoritative norms have been effaced, and this has come about by our own perverse agency; it's a case of self-inflicted nihilism. All that is left to us, culturally speaking, is to drift aimlessly through the void. The force of this text is not to make an argument about whether God exists or doesn't exist. It's a work of *cultural commentary*, describing a form of social life where *privileged horizons*, horizons that sustain a definite understanding of the point of human existence, have ceased to exist. The analysis is ultimately the same as the ones that have been sketched in the other four texts. Nietzsche the heroic atheist writes as if he is *nostalgic* about an era of committed pious belief precisely because a world where the idea of God has inconspicuously slipped away, virtually without anyone noticing or caring very much, betokens a world where robust horizons of life are too open-ended to be real horizons. And without real horizons of commitment and devotion, life is doomed to be incapable of being life-affirming. "Nostalgia" for some earlier cultural epoch of firm belief isn't the right way to put it. But the point is that he clearly experiences *dread* at what he sees as a present defined by horizonlessness and the loss of all definite anchors.

This theme is spelled out even more directly in the section immediately preceding the "madman" aphorism—namely, *Gay Science*, § 124: "*In the horizon of the infinite.*—We have left land and have embarked. We have burned our bridges behind us—indeed, we have gone farther and destroyed the land behind us. . . . There is nothing more terrifying [*nichts Furchtbareres*] than infinity." These are simply alternative images in order to convey the same teaching as that in § 125: the inevitable effect of modernity's banishing of all meaningful horizons is vertigo, anguish, and "homesickness" for the terra firma that has been foolishly conjured away. The obvious meaning of the aphorism's title is that a "horizon of the infinite" is precisely *not* a horizon.

The message from all these texts is clear: Nietzsche wanted creativity and open horizons for the heroic philosopher and wanted brutally closed and confined horizons for everyone else. His rhetoric often suggests that he wants openness and free-spiritedness for everyone. But in truth his view is that self-creation and unbounded horizons for everyone generates cultural catastrophe of unprecedented proportions. The democratic, bourgeois, post-Enlightenment world that he hated had, he thought, brought about precisely this epic cultural catastrophe. Nietzsche certainly anticipated that he would have a substantial following in the twentieth century. That he expected that this following would encompass a *mass readership* seems much more unlikely. People generally need to believe that the horizons defining their particular view of life are *true*. Therefore, communicating not just to spiritual elites but also to the demos at large that these horizons are *willed fabrications* seems counterproductive, to put it mildly. (In that sense, Nietzsche *really is*, despite his own intentions, contributing to the further radicalizing of open-horizoned cultural liberalization that he despised and warned against.)

In Nietzsche's view, people, to live life-affirming lives, need to live within very strict understandings of the purpose of life, and the more rigidly and authoritatively these horizons of existence get legislated, the better the prospects for a culture of self-affirmation and grandeur. Hence Nietzsche's emphatic theme of the connection between philosophers as the true elite and the imperative of ruling. "Genuine philosophers," he writes in *Beyond Good and Evil*, § 211, "are commanders and legislators: they say, 'thus it shall be!' They first determine the Whither and For What of man, and in so doing have at their disposal the preliminary labor of all philosophical laborers, all who have overcome the past. With a creative hand they reach for the future, and all that is and has been becomes a means for them, an instrument, a hammer. Their 'knowing' is creating, their creating is a legislation, their will to truth is—will to power."[39] Nietzsche wants to exalt philosophers to the highest rank of human beings, but at the same time he is determined to repudiate any ideal of philosophy as *contemplative*; philosophy, on the contrary, is presented as entirely oriented to *action*, to the reshaping of the world according to its superior insight, superior vitality, and superior will. The same conception can be traced all the way back to *Schopenhauer as Educator*: "Let us think of the philosopher's eye resting upon existence: he wants to determine its value anew. For it has been *the proper task of all great thinkers to be lawgivers* as to the measure, stamp and weight of things."[40] As he puts it near the end of that text, philosophers constitute the ultimate "tribunal."[41] A paltry, humanly unimpressive, and complacent culture—as all modern cultures are, in Nietzsche's view—would readily flatter itself that it is humanly adequate if genuine philosophers, with their ferocious will to truth cum will to power, didn't rise up to reassert higher standards of what it is to be human.

It is simply not the case that for Nietzsche, individuals constitute the meaning of their own lives for themselves, individual to individual, so to speak. Rather, meaning gets constituted (or doesn't get constituted) at the *cultural or civilizational* level. If the *culture* is horizonless, then *everyone* suffers from this horizonlessness, this lack of direction. Someone has to *take responsibility* for *legislating* these horizons of meaning—philosopher-kings, basically—and in Nietzsche's view, in the secularized, enlightened, and post-Christian dispensation of contemporary Europe, no one is taking that responsibility. Nineteenth-century European culture is not a culture but a pseudoculture, the absence of a culture. If Nietzsche actually thought that the problem of evaporated meaning that preoccupies him could be solved by individuals fashioning meaning in their own lives, why would he be so worked up about the state of the culture in modern Europe? But as we see from all these texts—and from countless other texts—Nietzsche is *very worked up indeed* about the state of the culture: its low ambitions, its lack of direction, and perhaps especially, its obliviousness to its own emptiness. (That is the real theme of the "madman" aphorism.) He says it clearly enough in the second of the *Untimely Meditations*: "Our modern culture is not a living thing. . . . *It is not a real culture at all but only a kind of knowledge of culture*; it has an idea of and feeling for culture but no true cultural achievement emerges from them."[42] He says that "the secret of modern culture" consists in the fact that "we moderns have nothing whatever of our own; only by replenishing and cramming ourselves with the ages, customs, arts, philosophies, religions, discoveries of others do we become anything worthy of notice, that is to say, walking encyclopaedias, which is what an ancient Greek transported into our own time would perhaps take us for."[43] For Nietzsche, the advent of modernity means, above all, the displacement of genuine cultures (which are all premodern) by mere pseudoculture, or at least the appreciation of past cultures as a replacement for the capacity to *produce* or *generate* authentic culture. Christianity as the ultimate boundary between antiquity and modernity is crucial to Nietzsche's narrative. This is in Nietzsche's view the true crime of Christianity and why he hates it so much. He spells this out in *Schopenhauer as Educator*, § 2: Christian morality presented itself as a higher morality than "antique virtue" and on that basis delegitimized and debunked ancient cultures as representing the peak of human possibilities. Once antiquity was associated with an inferior morality, culture as the ancients experienced it became utterly irrecoverable,[44] and the ultimate result of that debunking of pagan culture by Christianity is what comes to be known as "modernity."

In my view, the idea of Nietzsche as an unpolitical, antipolitical, or radically individualistic thinker is so far from being an adequate interpretation that I would be inclined to claim the very opposite: that the *whole* of Nietzsche's philosophy is subordinate to, or in the service of, his politics. That is, core Nietzschean doctrines such as eternal return or the will to power are specifically designed in order to contribute to the realization of his political philosophy[45]—an ultrareactionary political philosophy aimed at the discrediting of, and eventually the top-to-bottom transformation of, a post–French Revolution political order where, in Nietzsche's view, equality and social justice are simply euphemisms for European decline. (Some commentators on Nietzsche have actually gone so far as to suggest that there is simply no meaningful political philosophy in Nietzsche, but that's a patently absurd view.)

One last remark. It concerns the curious and somewhat bizarre fact that Nietzsche is widely celebrated as the very archetype of an "anti-foundationalist" and "post-metaphysical" style of philosophizing. All of that strikes me as nonsense. For sure, there's plenty of antimetaphysical and antifoundationalist *rhetoric* in Nietzsche's writings. But it doesn't survive scrutiny. There's a very explicit metaphysics in Nietzsche ("will to power"). Nietzsche takes as his starting point Schopenhauer's metaphysics. And he *revises it* in order to supplant what he sees as a fundamentally "life-denying" metaphysics with what he hopes is a supremely "life-affirming" metaphysics. What's "post-metaphysical" about that? On the contrary, what could be more metaphysical? (Heidegger at least gets *that* right!) As regards Nietzsche's supposed antifoundationalism, Nietzsche articulates a vision of the noble life that's intended to supply an *authoritative* normative standard for judging *all* human life. And if that view is correct, it provides the philosophical foundation for categorically rejecting centuries of historical experience. Again, what could be more foundationalist than that? In any case, that will be our topic for the next section.

Nietzsche's Preoccupation (Obsession) with Nobility

We suggested above that Nietzsche needed to polemicize against Christianity as viciously as he did because the utter discrediting of Christianity and its whole legacy for modern democratic culture was, in his view, a necessary requirement for a possible reversion to aristocratic human possibilities. If the undoing of egalitarianism and liberalism really is viable, what would the result of that colossal cultural revolution actually look like? What sort of project is one buying into when one buys into Nietzsche? Because there's so little *content* to Nietzsche's conception of nobility, he leaves it open to Nietzschean disciples or self-conceived disciples to deposit utterly base matter in the empty box outlined in his works (especially his late works). This is what the various fascists did. And despite what we might believe or hope, those fascists are still around and—arguably—growing in force in contemporary politics. As is evident throughout this book, I don't in any way assume that fascism has been safely consigned to the trash can of history, however much one may wish it were so.

I want to begin by commenting on a text from Nietzsche's last book, *Ecce Homo*. Leo Strauss, in an intellectual dialogue with Karl Löwith concerning Nietzsche, elaborated on Löwith's interpretation of Nietzsche by saying that Nietzsche's doctrine of eternal recurrence was intended to recapture the *serenity* of ancient political philosophy.[46] But because he developed these ideas in the context of a hyperpolemical confrontation with modernity, what was actually conveyed was not serenity but a kind of hysteria. To use Strauss's not unreasonable formulation, Nietzsche's advocacy on behalf of the ancients was not "calm" but "convulsive." I think that's fundamentally right, and it's very relevant indeed to what I'll have to say on the topic of Nietzsche and nobility. Thomas Mann, as quoted in a previous section, was equally right to say that as Nietzsche approached the completion of his literary output, his style and gestures became "shriller [and] more grotesque."[47]

In any case, Nietzsche writes (*Ecce Homo*, "Beyond Good and Evil," § 2) that *Beyond Good and Evil* "is in all essentials a critique of modernity," encompassing "the modern sciences, modern arts, and even modern politics." The purpose is to conjure up "a contrary type that is as little modern as possible—a noble, Yes-saying type."[48] What *defines* modernity is that it is decadent in the sense of life-denying or life-negating. Everything that defines modern culture, modern morality, and modern politics are in Nietzsche's perception simply different expressions of this fundamental nihilism or incapacity for life affirmation. Nobility, by contrast, is defined by its capacity to be life-affirming, to be yea-saying in the most comprehensive sense. In order for nobility in this sense to be possible, modernity must be defeated. We will know that we will have successfully emancipated ourselves from modernity (or are approaching the possibility of such emancipation) when nobility in that sense again becomes achievable. These interlocking propositions are at the very heart of Nietzsche's way of thinking.

We moderns define the culture of modernity according to a conception of egalitarian morality. We pride ourselves on it and regard it as emblematic of cultural superiority. Nietzsche famously reduces this morality to a psychology of resentment. Hence it is not something affirmative or positive but a negation masquerading as affirmation: supposed love of the good is really resentment of those who embody strength, healthiness, and the imperatives of power. As is well known, "genealogy" as Nietzsche practices it has been celebrated and embraced by the French intellectual left. But of course Nietzsche himself intended this genealogical philosophy as a root-and-branch intellectual destruction of "the left"—where, on Nietzsche's understanding, the left can be traced back not just to the French Revolution but to Plato's privileging of morality and idealism over the realities of power and self-assertion! There are two additional crucial texts from *Ecce Homo*, from §§ 2 and 4 of the "Birth of Tragedy" section of "Why I Write Such Good Books," that help crucially in appreciating the true nature of Nietzsche's project:

> I was the first to see the real opposition: the degenerating instinct that turns against life with subterranean vengefulness (Christianity, the philosophy of Schopenhauer, in a certain sense already the philosophy of Plato, and all of idealism as typical forms) versus a formula for the highest affirmation, born of fullness, of overfullness, a Yes-saying without reservation, even to suffering, even to guilt, even to everything that is

questionable and strange in existence. This ultimate, most joyous, most wantonly extravagant Yes to life represents not only the highest insight but also the deepest. . . . Nothing in existence may be subtracted, nothing is dispensable.[49]

Let us look ahead a century: let us suppose that my attempt to assassinate two millennia of antinature and desecration of man were to succeed. That new party of life which would tackle the greatest of all tasks, the attempt to raise humanity higher, including the relent-less destruction of everything that was degenerating and parasitical, would again make possible that *excess of life* on earth from which the Dionysian state, too, would have to awaken again. I promise a *tragic* age: the highest art in saying Yes to life, tragedy, will be reborn when humanity has weathered the consciousness of the hardest but most necessary wars *without suffering from it.*[50]

This is typical Nietzsche: the twentieth century will be a time of horrendous ideological war (true!). But this is cause not for abysmal anguish. On the contrary, this is cause almost for celebration; it will be a test of whether human beings of the twentieth century will have become the bearers of the kind of genuinely tragic culture that Nietzsche wants us to be. We have to tough our way through the deepest pessimism in order to arrive at the joyous yea-saying that awaits us at the far end of that deepest pessimism. If we fail the test, we are contemptible wimps and degenerates. If we pass the test, we will have proven ourselves to be creatures of a new species higher than a merely human one. The core idea is, again, that modernity precludes or disables the highest human possibilities because it renders inaccessible a tragic experience of life. Nobility = life-affirmation = grappling with the tragic character of existence and not being defeated by it but, on the contrary, *affirming* it in all its harshness; hence without tragedy, there is no nobility. Nietzsche, by virtue of offering a philosophy that opens up the possibility of a new "tragic age," thereby renders nobility possible again.

It would be a colossal mistake to interpret Nietzsche's talk of "nobility" as primarily animated by concern with the nobility of the individual self or the nobility of solitary artists and philosophers. No—the very first sentence of part 9 of *Beyond Good and Evil* refers to aristocratic *societies*—societies oriented toward aristocracy as a defining human possibility.[51] The same is emphatically the case in § 262, for instance: the emphasis is squarely on aristocratic *polities* and aristocratic *moralities*. Nobility becomes possible when we have *whole societies* that are comfortable with rank order, slavery, and oppression; that don't flinch from imposing their will with iron harshness; and that view their ultimate purpose as "an arrangement . . . for breeding."[52] I'd suggest that a month after reading the "What is Noble" section of *Beyond Good and Evil*, it is much easier to remember what Nietzsche says about the aristocratic characteristics of the kind of *society* that he thinks meets his standard than it is to remember what defines the personal traits of the kind of *individual* Nietzsche regards as a great-souled human being. That, it seems to me, is very telling. He's concerned with nobility both at the individual and societal level, but ask yourself which of these analyses is more memorable and easier to conceptualize.

Nietzsche's talk about slavery and exploitation as conditions of a meaningful culture is not what today gets referred to as a "dog whistle." It's a direct call to action. The project here is a resurrection of the ancien régime that ostensibly suffered permanent termination at the hands of the French Revolution. The rabble conquered "the last nobility of Europe," but the battle can be resumed; the victory of the former and the defeat of the latter can be reversed. There is no reason to think (so Nietzsche suggests) that the supposedly definitive moral revolution represented by "the ideas of 1789" is as final as was supposed. One needs to think in broader temporal horizons than a mere century or two; one lost the battle, but one can still win the war.

In an interesting exchange of emails concerning *Beyond Good and Evil*, § 262, a friend of mine, Loralea Michaelis, pointed out that Nietzsche, in this text, is more critical of aristocracy than I take him to be. Michaelis pointed out that his account there is somewhat reminiscent of Plato's account of the degeneration of the city in speech in the *Republic*. Here is my response: Yes, there's an account in *Beyond Good and Evil*, § 262, of the falling into decadence of aristocratic society. But the point of that account is not to criticize aristocracy. It culminates in a critique of Socrates and the Socratic "morality of mediocrity." (Simmel's "morality of nobility"[53] possibly alludes to this text, intending to present these two moralities as the fundamental philosophical alternatives for Nietzsche.) The question that he's asking is, How can a culture that's humanly so high nonetheless give rise to a champion of mediocrity like Socrates? Socratic-Platonic moralism = a lowering rather than raising of human possibilities. So how did an aristocratic culture allow that to happen? What decadence did it fall into such that it *could* happen? I agree that it's possible to see a parallel with Plato's story about the onset of the decadence of the kallipolis, and Nietzsche may even have deliberately intended that parallel. Plato's story is about *moral* decline, whereas Nietzsche's story is about decline measured by something higher than morality. It's tempting to read Nietzsche in a way that privileges philosophy over everything else; but it's telling that in this text, Socrates's status as the Ur-philosopher doesn't spare him from being judged by another standard—that of culture and nobility. It's as if Nietzsche is saying that the French Revolution's entrenchment of mediocrity began with Socrates and that Socrates's culpability on this score counts for more than his being the founder of the Western philosophical tradition. I think that is in fact Nietzsche's view—and perhaps Heidegger's as well.[54]

Nietzsche is indeed concerned with the nobility of the "higher man" in his singularity. But he is no less concerned with nobility or aristocracy as a *social* possibility—a possibility that modernity with its Christianity-inspired, and especially Reformation-inspired, embrace of democracy has annulled as a human possibility. Nietzsche's project is to revivify what the Reformation and the Enlightenment have seemingly put beyond acceptable moral bounds. An important reason behind Nietzsche's ambitious debunking of morality is that without the articulation of normative standards that *surpass* and *transcend* morality (the appeal to culture, to strength and vitality, and to nobility is intended to serve as precisely this articulation of a higher-than-morality standard!), humankind will remain stuck in what Nietzsche sees as the dehumanizing rut of a democratic cultural world that judges itself to be morally superior and therefore humanly superior.

To be sure, Nietzsche does concern himself with *the noble soul* as he understands it, and what distinguishes it from the ignoble soul. But he is *no less* concerned with the securing of a whole *culture* capable of keeping classes or castes separate, with each "knowing its place" and not aspiring to break down the boundaries between classes or castes. The very fact that Nietzsche is willing and eager to resurrect the language of "caste" (and also eager and willing to relegitimize the notion of slavery as a necessary feature of cultures superior to modern cultures!) tells one things that are absolutely crucial for rightly apprehending the character of what "critique of modernity" means in Nietzsche's thought.[55] "Modernity" means, among other things, a culture that refuses to tolerate the very notion of caste,[56] and to Nietzsche's way of thinking, this in itself explains why modernity is normatively perverse and must be destroyed. His work aims to commence this work of destruction by means of the intellectual resuscitation of notions that modernity had presumed itself to have definitively conquered.

For Nietzsche, the vulgarity of modern culture is encapsulated in the fact that it is a culture based on the reading of newspapers. He highlights this in the preface to *Beyond Good and Evil*, in § 263, as well as in *Schopenhauer as Educator*. Why does he put so much emphasis on this? Because newspapers presuppose that everyone in the society reacts to the same events and makes judgments on the same social phenomena and everything is interchangeable across all ranks of society.[57] It is the mark of a uni-class social world. He despises that! In §§ 56–57 of his late text, *The Antichrist*, Nietzsche ecstatically praises *The Book of Manu*, the ancient Hindu lawbook. In weighing the significance of that praise, it's worth considering this passage from a book on contemporary India: "Death was the sentence to an untouchable who wanted an education. The Laws of Manu, followed by orthodox Hindus, prescribed the method of execution. If an untouchable even overheard Sanskrit, the language of the scriptures, he was to be killed by having molten lead poured into his ears."[58] That is so unspeakably extreme that when we read it, our natural reaction is to think that Nietzsche couldn't possibly have been serious in celebrating the laws of ancient Hinduism. But that's wrong. When we read *Beyond Good and Evil*, § 263, we realize that for Nietzsche, precisely a law or cultural norm like that captures something essential about what is fundamentally right about ancient cultures and correspondingly, what is utterly wrong with modern cultures: the norm of all citizens relating to each other by reading the same newspapers (or today, watching the same TV programs) makes the same point from the opposite end, so to speak. Related to this is Nietzsche's idea of nobility as aversion to being contaminated with what's unclean, as we see very clearly from his discussion of "pollution" both in § 263 and in § 271: "The baseness of some people suddenly spurts up like dirty water when some holy vessel, some precious thing from a locked shrine . . . is carried past. . . . The masses . . . are not to touch everything; . . . there are holy experiences before which they have to take off their shoes and keep away their unclean hands." What defined the chandala class in ancient Hinduism was not just being low but being "unclean," polluted, or capable of "contaminating" what is holy with what is unclean, and clearly there are equivalents to these notions in many or most world religions. Again, Nietzsche sees these as the marks of *noble* cultures, as opposed to the vulgar culture of modernity. (And one should not fail to ask, If Nietzsche found the *nineteenth* century vulgar, what would he have thought of the twenty-first century?) When he bemoans the condition of "secularization" in *Schopenhauer as Educator*, this is an important part of what he has in mind.[59] Notwithstanding his avowed atheism, in Nietzsche's eyes modernity is not *vindicated* but on the contrary *condemned* by the fact that it progressively banishes such notions.

The more one familiarizes oneself with the repellent discourse of the contemporary extreme right, the easier it becomes to pick up distinct echoes of Nietzschean themes and imagery. For instance, it is very hard to read Goodrick-Clarke's book on neo-Nazi cults, *Black Sun*, without being struck again and again by how Nietzsche's work supplies—and is understood by such ideologues as supplying[60]—an abundant reservoir of defining mythological tropes for these neo-Nazis: how he refers to "we Hyperboreans" at the start of *The Antichrist*; how he describes the *Book of Manu* as an "absolutely *Aryan* work" in a letter to Peter Gast dated May 31, 1888; how he talks about a return to slavery and a new caste system; how he tries to fan the sparks of a neopagan revival; how he denounces Judaism and Christianity as slave religions and castigates the Jewish origins of Christianity; how he resurrects Zoroaster as a symbol of anti-Christianity and mythicizes about cosmic cycles; and especially how he offers prophecies of a race of supermen who will rescue Europe from the curse of egalitarianism.

Let's consider again the magnificent Tocqueville text cited in the introduction: "Equality is perhaps less elevated; but it is more just, and its justice makes for its greatness and its beauty."[61] Tocqueville shared Nietzsche's worries about the cultural effects of an age that decided to break sharply with aristocracy. (There's a lot of proto-Nietzscheanism packed into Tocqueville's potent line about the "petty and vulgar pleasures" of an egalitarian culture.[62]) But in Tocqueville's view equality was nonetheless not just *historically inevitable* (which it may or may not be) but *normatively mandatory.* The Tocquevillean acknowledgment of egalitarian justice is a quote that every reader of Nietzsche should cleave tightly to his or her bosom. We need it to ward off what's most perilous in Nietzsche's thought, precisely because Tocqueville seeks to address head-on precisely those cultural concerns that fundamentally animate Nietzsche. (Without doubt, Nietzsche would dismiss it as another case of a noble soul being blinded or hoodwinked by Christianity.) Nietzsche makes clear in *Beyond Good and Evil,* part 9 and elsewhere, that in his view *justice* on the contrary is aligned with *rank order and hierarchy,* and only a civilization corrupted by Christianity, and especially Protestant Christianity, would see things otherwise. I don't believe that Nietzsche ever explains *why* a hierarchical society is more just than an egalitarian one. However, I very much suspect that he would say that if this is something that you need to have *explained* to you, that already shows that you have a thoroughly corrupted view of life.

Finally, I want to consider to what extent Nietzsche himself lives up to the standards he articulates in *Beyond Good and Evil*. Let's start with Nietzsche's articulation in § 292 of what it is to be a philosopher: "a person who constantly experiences, sees, hears, suspects, hopes, and dreams extraordinary things; who is struck by his own thoughts as if from outside, from above and below, as if by his type of events and lightning bolts; who is perhaps a storm himself. . . . a fatal person in whose vicinity things are always rumbling, growling, gaping, and acting in uncanny ways." I think it would be easy to obtain a consensus that Nietzsche fairly readily passes that test with respect to whether or not he is a philosopher.

But he does *not* so readily pass another test—namely, how he stands in relation to the two fundamentally opposed alternatives that it is the purpose of *Beyond Good and Evil*, part 9, to lay out: nobility and resentment. Nietzsche is a tireless champion of ideals of nobility, but where is the nobility in Nietzsche's writings as he himself defines it? Nobility is associated with a stance toward life that is joyously affirmative and comprehensively yea-saying. But Nietzsche's prose in *Beyond Good and Evil* and in other writings that we have surveyed here, as well as in countless other writings that we have not surveyed, seems aggressively polemical and resentful, expressing no little anger and hostility directed against his standard targets: against women; against Germans whose Lutheran Reformation proved them to be fundamentally plebeian; against liberals; against egalitarians of all stripes; against the subpar intellectuals who teach philosophy in the universities; against the intellectual culture of the 1880s that ignores him and doesn't feel any world-historical obligation to read his books; against the democratic "rabble" who touch things that they have no right to touch and judge things that they have no right to judge (*Beyond Good and Evil*, § 263); and so on. (My colleague Ed Andrew has rightly suggested to me that Nietzsche put lots of energy into exposing liberal and leftist resentment, but he turned a blind eye toward, or was silent about, the resentments of the right, including his own.) His rage is such that Donald Trump starts looking like a model of civility and thoughtfulness relative to the rants and rancor expressed throughout Nietzsche's oeuvre. For Nietzsche, nobility and resentment must be judged relative to each other—nobility as a stance toward life focused on its own inner grandeur and richness, resentment as a stance toward life focused on that outside itself that it hates and against which it seeks revenge. Which of these polar alternatives ultimately predominates in how Nietzsche fashions his texts?[63]

Here's another question worth pondering: How is it that a philosopher with such a harshly reactionary view of life could come to cast such a spell on so many towering thinkers of the following century? That's the question I want to pursue in my reflections on Nietzsche and his legacy in the closing section of this chapter.

Chapter 1

Nietzsche's Heirs: Freud and Weber

I want to begin this section with a quotation from Karl Jaspers because I think it helps clarify why it might be worth taking a little excursus into the question of how Nietzsche, with his rhetoric extolling tragedy and a possible return to pagan horizons, sets the agenda for Sigmund Freud and Max Weber: "Christian salvation opposes tragic knowledge. The chance of being saved destroys the tragic sense of being trapped without chance of escape. Therefore no genuinely Christian tragedy can exist. For in Christian plays, the mystery of redemption is the basis and framework of the plot, and the tension of tragic knowledge has been released from the outset with the experience of man's perfection and salvation through grace. At this point, tragedy loses its compelling character."[64] The point here is not whether an ambitious case could be made for Jaspers's thesis but whether it captures an important aspect of Nietzsche's animus against Christianity, an animus then to some extent bequeathed to Freud and Weber.

A founding premise of much of Nietzsche's philosophy (including his political philosophy) is the idea of the ignobility of worldviews that presuppose ultimate metaphysical unity or metaphysical harmony, relative to views of life that demand heroic willing or resolute decisionism in the midst of tragic conflict. This accounts for Nietzsche's basic hostility toward Plato and also accounts for his thesis that Christianity is fundamentally a popularized version of Platonism (*Beyond Good and Evil*, preface). Here, simply reproduced from a previous book of mine,[65] is a summary of some relevant texts:

Firstly: Nietzsche's attack, extending from *The Birth of Tragedy* to *Twilight of the Idols*, on the Socratic (rationalist) tradition as an *anti-tragic* tradition, which Nietzsche casts as an issue of tragic depth versus shallow rationalism. Secondly: Nietzsche's insistence, in *Genealogy of Morals*, First Essay, section 1, on the existence of "plain, harsh, ugly, repellent, unchristian, immoral truth," in order to challenge the Platonic-Christian presumption of the metaphysical unity of truth, beauty, and goodness. Thirdly: Nietzsche's indictment of Plato for having "destroyed paganism," and correspondingly, for his "preparation of the soil for Christianity"[66]—that is, for having helped a fundamentally ignoble view of life displace a fundamentally noble one.

The rejections of Christianity and gestures toward neopaganism that one finds in countless versions of neofascist ideology in the twentieth and twenty-first centuries (right up to the present day) are simply vulgar-Nietzschean echoes of these serious philosophical claims. But interestingly, these claims are not only echoed in contemporary vulgar-Nietzschean ideologies; they are also echoed in powerful and sophisticated thinkers such as Sigmund Freud and Max Weber. Freud, Weber, and Heidegger represent the three most intellectually ambitious post-Nietzschean thinkers, and quite tellingly, Nietzsche's rhetoric impugning Christianity as effete and cowardly had a major impact on all three of them.

***

At the end of § 2 of *Schopenhauer as Educator*, Nietzsche refers to Schopenhauer's "heirs" (*seinen Erben*).[67] He clearly has in mind people like himself—people of the same intellectual stature as Schopenhauer and for whom the example of Schopenhauer will be inspiring with respect to what is possible in the way of a genuinely philosophical life. It's not a question of Schopenhauer's specific arguments or specific metaphysical doctrines—Nietzsche seems to have astonishingly little to say about any of that. What captivates him is the *ideal of life* that for him is represented by Schopenhauer as a singular practitioner of philosophy as a mode of life superior to other modes of life (he tends to exalt the trinity of *philosopher, artist, saint,* with all other existential possibilities located infinitely far below these). But he is likely not only gesturing toward himself as a bona fide heir of Schopenhauer; if *he* is the Schopenhauer of the late nineteenth century, he is no less gesturing toward *"the heirs of Nietzsche"* who will carry the same ideals of fearless and world-transforming philosophical life praxis forward into the twentieth century. As *he* stands in relation to *Schopenhauer,* so *others* will eventually stand in relation to *him.* That raises the question of who these others will be and how they will adapt and carry forward the Nietzschean legacy. So here I want to offer a brief sketch of ways in which the two key ideas that I have zeroed in on as defining the *core* of Nietzsche's intellectual/political concerns (especially the idea of tragedy and how it defines nobility) are also strikingly present in Freud and Weber (Heidegger too, but we'll reserve Heidegger for the next chapter).

Let's start with the famous "gods and demons" notion proposed by Weber. Weber, in "Science as a Vocation," presents monotheism as a distortion or obfuscation of the "natural" experience of human beings. The "default position," one might say, is polytheism. He quotes John Stuart Mill to that effect, and he powerfully endorses it.[68] The gods are many, and we human beings have to decide, with resolve, commitment, and ultimately courage, which of those gods to serve, defer to, or try to ingratiate ourselves with. On reflection, there is something here quite similar to (one might say it's an alternative way of formulating) Nietzsche's essential idea of the modern horizonlessness of human beings, the devastating cultural effects of that horizonlessness, and the corresponding need to impose or reimpose horizons of sustainable meaning upon ourselves. God is dead, rational standards of how to live one's life are dead, metaphysics is dead, and hence *the burden is now on us* to come up with viable horizons. We stare in the face the abyss of meaning into which the last two millennia of Western rationalism have thrust us and somehow we must identify workable means by which to survive it. Weber's conception of the competing gods and demons that jostle with each other in pursuit of our total allegiance—gods and demons to which we commit ourselves without any appeal to the authority of reason or the authority of religious traditions or any other authoritative normative standard—is a version of Nietzsche's project of legislating authoritative horizons whose only authority is the act of legislation itself.

Interestingly, Freud too concludes *Civilization and Its Discontents* with a stern account of *warring gods* locked in a mortal struggle for domination. He too writes scathingly about what he sees as the sentimentalism and naiveté of Christian morality. He too echoes Nietzsche's rhetoric about staring harsh truths square in the eye and not flinching. In fact, pervasive in all three—Nietzsche,

Weber, Freud—is a conception of the higher nobility of a tragic view of life and the fundamental ignobility of thinking that the world is more welcoming to human beings than it really is (an ignobility crucially encouraged by Christianity).

We have already made reference to the famous quote from the preface to *Beyond Good and Evil*: Christianity is "Platonism for the people"; Christianity is Platonism democratized. But what does this formula mean? What's involved in democratizing Platonism? What aspect of Plato or Platonism gets fed into the whole Western moral and cultural tradition via the vehicle of the Christian religion? Nietzsche doesn't even begin to provide elaboration. It's evocative and memorable, but surely more content has to be sketched in. Let me attempt to do that, since I think it will prove to be helpful in getting insight (or starting to get insight) into the "Nietzschean" dimensions of Freud and Weber.

Central to Nietzsche's view of what's wrong with the Socratic-Platonic origins of Western philosophy is the "Platonic" affirmation of ultimate metaphysical harmony: apprehension of what's true fundamentally converges with or is in alignment with experience of what's beautiful, which in turn fundamentally converges with or is in alignment with the practice of what's good. We inhabit a kind of "ontological triangle" (truth/beauty/goodness) that's in fundamental harmony with itself. The universe is in some ultimate sense at peace with itself. Nietzsche's view is that this not only does violence to our actual experience of reality; more important, perhaps, it contributes decisively to the "anti-tragic" character of Christianity that has—according to its long-term effects—rendered our culture so shallow. Heidegger, I hope to show in the next chapter, profoundly agrees with that diagnosis. At the beginning of this section, I cited some texts to attest to the fact that that is Nietzsche's view and that attacking "Platonic" metaphysics is a crucial component of Nietzsche's larger philosophical and cultural project, but there are plenty of other such texts. Moreover, it's interesting and important to appreciate to what extent Freud and Weber go along with, or sympathize with, that aspect of Nietzsche's agenda or project.

Consider a short text by Weber entitled "Between Two Worlds."[69] Especially telling is the emphatic appeal to the language of "fate": the German *Machtstaat* must face down the Russians. "That is fate, and no amount of pacifist talk will alter the fact." Germany, with its "tragic historical obligations," cannot conduct itself as if it were Switzerland, for to do so would display blindness with respect to "our particular fate."[70] Weber is famous for his doctrine of the obligatory commitment to "value-freedom" in the social sciences. Is this a "value-free" text? Certainly not. There are two "worlds," one "honorable" and the other conspicuously "dishonorable." Weber makes pretty clear that in his view Switzerland doesn't have the "guts" to bear the world-historical burden of state power exercised by Germany. Again, there is nothing value-free in that message. And it's entirely consistent with the normative message that runs through the two "Vocation" lectures. But if it's normative rather than value-free, what kind of moral universe is conjured up by Weber? Even if Weber isn't Nietzsche (and let's be clear: he isn't), Weber's moral world overlaps in important ways with Nietzsche's moral world. It's a world of *fate*; of *tragedy and tragic responsibility*; of *courage and manliness*; of *resoluteness and resolute masculinity*; of *strength, heroism, existential pathos*, rock-hard *fidelity to one's own chosen values*. Above all, Weber's moral world demonstrates the imperative to exhibit *nobility* in bearing the tragic burden of life and its tough choices. It's a grim but noble destiny. Life is harsh, the choices on offer are starkly unbridgeable, and heroism is required simply in order to decide which of the various worldviews to embrace. In short, it's a small philosophical leap from Nietzsche to Weber (and also a small philosophical leap from Weber to the existentialists—and also to Carl Schmitt). Weber has a detached social-science rhetoric and he has his courage and nobility rhetoric, and the two rhetorics are, to put it mildly, flat-out contradictory.

Before concluding the discussion of Freud and Weber, let me quote another text from Weber that helps to clarify why Weber admires Nietzsche to the extent that he does. (It's obviously related to the "courage and nobility rhetoric" in Weber to which I just referred.) "Nietzsche occasionally gives voice to the conception of the 'artist-god' with the negative moralistic pathos which often betrays an embarrassing residue of bourgeois philistinism even in some of his greatest passages. Its intention was to expressly renounce any 'meaning' of the empirical world. A powerful, and at the same time kind, God could not have created such a world. Only a villain could have done so."[71] Here's my gloss. For millennia, human beings had tolerated the idea of a God who was presumed to be both just and all-powerful as if it were a plausible idea. It's *not* a plausible idea. And Nietzsche had been the one who had the courage to announce more clearly than anyone else that it's not a plausible idea. Weber seems to be saying that this gives anyone who considers himself or herself to be a serious thinker sufficient reason to take Nietzsche as their starting point.

***

I want to end this chapter with some sobering thoughts from Leo Strauss, as related by the biographer of Canada's leading conservative political thinker, George Grant. Grant conceived the idea for the radio lectures on the thought of Nietzsche that became Grant's book, *Time as History*, and apparently consulted Strauss about the wisdom of introducing Nietzsche to a mass audience. Here is Strauss's view as reported in the Grant biography:

> Leo Strauss strongly believed that Nietzsche was a writer of such intoxicating destructiveness that he should not be discussed in the presence of people without philosophic training: his ideas might do them harm. Strauss agreed entirely with George about Nietzsche's central importance, but he thought it more prudent to attack his epigones like Weber and Freud, rather than confront the master directly . . . "Strauss said that Nietzsche had a right to think what he thought, [but] it was dubious if he ever should have written it down, and it was even further dubious that he should have ever published it."[72]

Admittedly, we are getting Strauss's judgment on Nietzsche second- or third-hand; still, it is not at all hard to believe that this faithfully conveys what Strauss said to Grant. I'll offer a two-part commentary. First, what Strauss says about Weber and Freud is, for me, more shocking than what he says about Nietzsche. I'm fully committed to the notion that Freud and Weber owe a large intellectual debt to Nietzsche that isn't widely enough acknowledged or thought through, so I'm certainly receptive to Strauss's suggestion about the tacit Nietzscheanism of these two thinkers. But "epigones" who one can attack as proxies for "the master"! That's a bit outrageous. These were two towering thinkers of our age, and however profoundly they were shaped by the imperative to engage intellectually with the challenge of Nietzsche, they were certainly not mere epigones. (Of course, Strauss didn't necessarily use the word "epigones": it might have been George Grant's gloss on Strauss, or even William Christian's gloss on Grant.)

Here is my second comment: Nietzsche is part of the cultural air we breathe. The culture and intellectual life of the last hundred years are unthinkable without him. So the suggestion that all of that should have been kept to merely private musings in Nietzsche's own head seems staggering. But there's a real truth in Strauss's conception of the "intoxicating destructiveness" in Nietzsche, and I would go so far as to say that anyone who reads Nietzsche without anxiety about his potential dangerousness is at some fundamental level failing to take Nietzsche seriously. For me, it's time to "square accounts" with Nietzsche (who, as I mentioned at the start of this chapter, I was quite absorbed by in my youth). But squaring accounts with him largely means being forthright about how dangerous he is. The free play of ideas obviously counts for a lot within the broader economy of human life, which is why we have good reason to accord substantial latitude to philosophers vis-à-vis the sober purposes of society writ large. But the moral and political responsibility of intellectuals also matters a lot, which is why it's important not to lose sight of the difference between latitude and license.

There is a kind of insane recklessness to Nietzsche—as if nothing he could write, no matter how irresponsible, no matter how inflammatory, could possibly do any harm. All that matters is *raising the stakes*, and there is no such thing as raising the stakes *too high*. That brings us back to our epigraph at the head of this chapter, drawn from a June 1884 letter written by Nietzsche to Malwida von Meysenbug: "The sort of unqualified and utterly unsuitable people who may one day come to invoke my authority is a thought that fills me with dread."[73] Well, if Nietzsche was so terrified about this (*macht mir der Gedanke Schrecken*), why didn't he simply exercise more responsibility or more prudence about how he wrote? *There's no good answer to this question.* It's as if Nietzsche were saying, I have to be true to my philosophy even if the consequence is utter ruin and havoc. Articulation of my truths, releasing them into the world, is so humanly important that it trumps all prudence and sanity, which appear unimportant by comparison. As I say, there is a kind of extreme lunacy to the view that all that matters is raising the stakes and that there is no such thing as raising the stakes too high. Nietzsche has elevated the civilizational responsibility of the philosopher to such sublime (= insane) heights that the norm of responsibility itself goes right out the window. The pathos borne by the heroic philosopher is impressive, but it is a pathos bought at an absurdly high price.

Chapter 2

Reading Heidegger in an
Age of Resurgent Fascism

> Heidegger . . . claims to be engaged, as the passive yet
> resonant medium of destiny, in the preparation of
> "another beginning," or a return to the original mani-
> festation of Being to the archaic Greek thinkers and
> poets. . . . [T]he end of metaphysics, . . . of which the
> last is the mature teaching of Nietzsche, is the sign of
> future salvation, a sign that is incarnated in Heidegger
> as the second coming. We should not begrudge Hei-
> degger the assumption of the robes of prophecy. This
> is after all a costume that has been irresistible to all
> the great thinkers of our race. We must nevertheless
> beware of false prophets.
>
> —Stanley Rosen

I have no doubt that there are many good, thoughtful,
and decent human beings who sincerely believe that Martin Heidegger has indispensable things to teach us and

that recognition of Heidegger's intellectual preeminence requires us to bracket some of the most questionable aspects of his thought and biography. As a consequence, many good and well-meaning Western intellectuals have done their utmost to give the benefit of the doubt to a great philosopher who in fact was *not* a decent human being. Over the decades, much has come to light that is very disturbing about Heidegger—not least the pattern of dishonesty in how he presented himself in the years following the defeat of the Nazi regime. This would perhaps be a manageable problem if it were possible to draw a clear and firm line between Heidegger the thinker and Heidegger the human being; but as one rereads his work in the light of what we now know about his deeds and character, that line has become harder and harder to sustain. It might be appropriate to cite Marx's acute maxim: "One basis for life and another basis for science is a priori a lie."[1] Recent books (including, but not limited to, Emmanuel Faye's *Heidegger: The Introduction of Nazism into Philosophy*) have shown that Heidegger's Nazism penetrated much more deeply into his philosophy than was commonly believed, and the controversies surrounding publication of the *Black Notebooks* have driven home that awareness with even greater decisiveness.[2] Even more worryingly, we see much in recent events that give us ample reason to fear that the fascist episode in modern politics is not over. Hence this might be the appropriate time finally to accept that Heidegger the human being, and hence Heidegger the philosopher, is tainted beyond repair. One notable left-Heideggerian—namely, Fred Dallmayr—says that his work on Heidegger is animated by a desire "to build a bridge between Freiburg and Frankfurt."[3] If the reading of Heidegger that follows is on the mark, I'm afraid that there can be no such bridge. In his 1993 book on Heidegger, Dallmayr also avows that when he read the *Letter on Humanism* for the first time, he was pleasantly surprised to find it "untainted by any of the sinister pronouncements I had expected."[4] Well, I truly wish that were the case, but sinister pronouncements are not lacking in this text, as we will see below. The question I'm raising in this chapter is whether, finding ourselves now in a political landscape where the possibility increasingly looms of Heidegger as a potential resource for the far right,[5] it might be best for left Heideggerianism (a paradox to begin with) to close up shop.

Aleksandr Dugin's Heidegger

When a representative of the contemporary far right such as Aleksandr Dugin reads Heidegger, what does he absorb as the pertinent political-cultural message? In *Martin Heidegger: The Philosophy of Another Beginning*, Dugin subsumes Heidegger's philosophy under what he calls "the political ideology of the Third Way."[6] What is "the Third Way"? It was an intellectual movement—which Dugin also refers to as "the Conservative Revolution"— that arose primarily in Germany in the wake of Germany's defeat in the First World War defined by equal rejection of Marxism in the East and "'Americanism' and, broadly speaking, Anglo-Saxon Liberalism ('planetary idiocy') in the West."[7] Membership included such thinkers as Oswald Spengler, Carl Schmitt, Othmar Spann, Fredrich and Ernst Jünger, Arthur Moeller van den Bruck, Ludwig

Klages, and many others. These were thinkers, needless to say, who cultivated the cultural ground that bred fascist and Nazi politics and who are still widely read on the far right.[8] Clearly, it was "third way" in relation to liberal democracy as the first way and communism as the second way. Dugin's project is to return, intellectually and ideologically, to this world of the German far right of the 1920s, and to resume their political enterprise before it went a little haywire with the Nazis:

> Heidegger was . . . an integral part of this movement. He was a "conservative revolutionary" in the sense that, as he understood it, man was called upon to . . . take a risky leap into another Beginning (the "Revolutionary" moment). . . . The Conservative Revolution in Germany and its counterparts in other European countries, notably in Italy, Spain, etc., were that very ideological environment in which Fascism and National Socialism—Third-Way ideologies—sprung up. . . . The main object of criticism from the leaders of the Conservative Revolution was the spirit of Modernity and its most striking manifestations: individualism and rationalism, utilitarianism, dogmatism, materialism, subjectivism—in other words, [First Way] *nihilism* and [Second Way] *Machenschaft* [machination].[9]

This is obviously an ideological appropriation of Heidegger. But it is an ideological appropriation to which Heidegger's philosophy quite readily lends itself. To be sure, Heidegger and those philosophically/ideologically akin to him did not get the destruction of modernity that they were hoping for from fascism and Nazism. Many of them (including Heidegger, eventually) recoiled from "compromising" with the "vulgarity, populism, and unprincipled pragmatism [!] of Hitler's Party."[10] Of course, they were aristocrats and the Nazis were plebeians. The fact that Dugin in this text is able to rebuke Nazism on account of its "unprincipled pragmatism" (implying that Heidegger's version of National Socialism, subscribed to by Dugin, was "principled" in a way that Hitler's wasn't!) might help to clarify why Dugin in another striking text issues a stirring call for a more purely and authentically "fascist fascism."[11]

Available on various Russian propaganda websites, including Dugin's own 4PT website, one can find an interview with Dugin on the topic of Heidegger, which is indeed quite illuminating for those interested in penetrating the smoke screen of Dugin's supposed "philosophy."[12] What follows is my brief summary of what Dugin says in that interview. *Dasein = Volk.* Heidegger could only criticize the Nazis from within the Nazi Party because criticisms of Nazism deriving from other ideologies are more contaminated by modernity than Nazism is and hence lack validity. The defining sin of liberal society is that it lacks rootedness in an ethnos ("artificial societies that have broken ties with their ethnic base"). Heidegger can affirm the "metaphysical destiny" of the German *Volk*, and Dugin can affirm the "metaphysical destiny" of Russia, without either of them counting as a vulgarly modern "nationalist." Similarly, one can be a fervent anti-Semite, as Heidegger was and as Dugin is, without counting as a racist.[13] The liberal West is approaching its final Eschaton, and the Greek Logos will be reborn in Russia, after

Dugin's conservative revolution definitively overthrows liberal barbarism. Heidegger as a *völkisch* fascist can only be understood by fellow *völkisch* fascists. Heidegger will be capable of being understood once the world undergoes transformation by a new, *purer* (i.e., less modern) fascist dispensation.[14] What is especially striking to me in this neofascist *defense* of Heidegger is how closely it matches the account of him that we get from penetrating critics of Heidegger's philosophy such as Charles Bambach and Emmanuel Faye.

The Challenge of Heidegger

The question of Heidegger's relationship to National Socialism has not gone away. On the contrary, in important ways, the question of that relationship has over time (including quite recently) become much more intense. Why is that? Well, it's a widely held view (not universal, but widely held) that Heidegger was *the* most important philosopher of the twentieth century. That's a credible view of his importance. Yet he very publicly endorsed just about the most barbaric political movement that has ever existed, aligned himself with that movement in a very active way for at least one year, did so in a less active way probably for something like fifteen years (1930–1945),[15] and never expressed an ounce of regret or contrition, though he was urged to do so by many who were close to him.[16] We generally expect philosophy to contribute to wisdom at least on the part of philosophers themselves. Heidegger, through his misguided political commitment, not only significantly discredited his *own* philosophy;

arguably, he contributed to the discrediting of philosophy as such.

Someone *might* say that Heidegger was a great philosopher but had nothing of interest or importance to contribute with respect to *political philosophy*. One might say that, but personally, that would not be my view. My view would be that with someone offering as intellectually ambitious and encompassing a philosophy as we get from Heidegger, there *has* to be a political philosophy as well. And indeed there is. On Heidegger's view, we are provided with a *political* standard for judging the worth of different cultures or different civilizations by considering to what extent those cultures or civilizations measure up to the question of Being, the question of what it means to be—not "what does it mean for you or me to be?" but "what does it mean for *beings or entities in general* to be?" According to Heidegger, some cultures are *attuned* to that question, make it present to us, bring us into closer proximity to it; other cultures obscure it, hide it, encourage us to forget about it. On Heidegger's view, we are today living in a civilization—liberal modernity—that represents the most woeful abyss with respect to the question of *what it means for beings to be*—that is, for the whole amazing variety of beings that we know to "have" being to "come forth," as opposed to being frozen in nonbeing, as it were. One can imagine eternal nothingness. But the world we have isn't eternal nothingness; it's a plentitude of being. Why isn't that at the center of our attention? Why do we devote so much energy to all the trivial and banal things that occupy us from day to day and so little attention or energy to the astonishing fact of being? Why don't our cultures imbue us with this wonder at the reality that the world is being and not nothingness? On Heidegger's view, this is a cultural/political/metaphysical catastrophe, and we have to trace this catastrophe back to its roots, in the history of philosophy commencing with Plato. There will ultimately be over a hundred volumes in the Heidegger *Collected Works* in German, no doubt because he thinks it takes that scale of intellectual exertion in order to do the indispensable work of diagnosis and criticism.

Heidegger's hope was that this "oblivion of Being" could be overcome by a root-and-branch destruction of liberal modernity under the guidance of German hyper-nationalism in the 1930s. We all know that that path led to mind-boggling genocide and the utter destruction of civilized life in Europe. Maybe Heidegger would say that what was at stake required us to roll the dice on that and that there was no guarantee that the dice roll would give us what was desired. A similar challenge, of course, could be put to Nietzsche. But by what authority did they think that they could authorize or legitimize a dice roll that could have those consequences? Who elected them as civilizational philosopher-kings? From Heidegger, who lived to see the consequences of a thoroughgoing annulment of Western egalitarianism and humanitarianism, of freedom and decency, we didn't get even a modest apology.

There are affinities and also important differences between Heidegger's philosophical project and Nietzsche's. We should sketch both. With respect to the differences, Nietzsche dismissed nationalism under the rubric of "petty politics," and whatever vague and probably crazy ideas he might have had with respect to "grand politics" (*große Politik*), what he was yearning for was significantly different from what Heidegger was yearning for.

The German *Volk*, for Nietzsche, was not the solution.[17] But with respect to the diagnosis, the parallels between Nietzsche and Heidegger are indeed overwhelming. For both, Plato and Socratic-Platonic rationalism are the ultimate culprits behind the movement of banalization and modernity's relentless tendency to render human existence utterly shallow. For both of them, Christianity was a disaster, and whatever was wrong with the history of Western metaphysics was made incomparably worse by the fact that our civilization is a civilization thoroughly shaped by Christianity. According to Heidegger, the last major culture to be properly "attuned" to the question of Being (and that had the *cultural and existential depth* that flows from being capable of measuring up to that question) was the tragic culture of the pre-Socratic, pre-Platonic Greeks. Nietzsche doesn't use the same vocabulary and doesn't express his central idea in the language of the question of Being, but his view was basically the same.

What do we make of Heidegger's megalomaniacal philosophical project? Let me begin with three quick points: First, if there was nothing to the question of Being that Heidegger defines as the center of his philosophy, it's impossible that Heidegger would have had the enormous cultural impact and philosophical influence that he has undoubtedly had. Second, a question: Did Heidegger really need to write a hundred volumes of philosophy in order to put this back on the agenda? There's something truly *insane* in that kind of manic intellectual activity. And third, however insane it may have been to inflate his philosophical concerns to the gargantuan proportions that he did, it was *far more insane* to think that these reflections in the realm of metaphysics, and the history of metaphysics, directly generated political prescriptions—and not just conventional political prescriptions but revolutionary imperatives of such force that it was legitimate for them to trump all foregoing standards of justice, morality, civility, and political sanity. In this respect at least, Heidegger was the most direct, most important, and most catastrophic of Nietzsche's many intellectual heirs.

There was a point at which it might have been possible for Heidegger's defenders to say that while Heidegger was indeed a committed German nationalist, and notwithstanding his direct complicity during the first year of the Nazi regime, the real Nazi in the Heidegger household was not Martin but Elfride;[18] that unlike Frau Heidegger, he wasn't an anti-Semite; and that in any case one could hive off his philosophy from his misguided political commitments. The facts that have come to light concerning Heidegger in recent decades have steadily diminished the credibility of such defenses, and we now know that they don't hold up. True, Heidegger rejected the biologistic ideology of the Nazis (*which doesn't mean that he rejected anti-Semitism*). But he truly believed in the greatness of Hitler and truly believed that the Nazi movement, under the leadership of Hitler, had the cultural power to plumb the depths of the mystery of Being in a way that liberal democracies were utterly incapable of doing.[19] That is, he believed that the experience of the self-revelation of Being that the Greeks were plugged into before Socrates and Plato came on the scene—and that was closed to the 2,500-year history of metaphysics but recovered with tantalizing brevity in the life and poetry and neopagan yearnings of Hölderlin—could be put within reach once again by a Nazi-ruled Europe. That's

not just a mistake (we all make mistakes). That's an enduring stain on the philosophy of Heidegger, and it proves
that, notwithstanding all the rhetoric of humility that runs
throughout the oeuvre of Heidegger, in the final reckon-
ing his megalomania far exceeds his humility.

Pre-Nazi Heidegger: The Being-toward-Death Chapter of *Being and Time*

It's impossible to make judgments about the political
dimensions of Heidegger's thinking without first making
some effort to penetrate what his philosophy is about. A
ready way of doing the latter is to take a look at what is
arguably the decisive text of early Heidegger—namely,
Being and Time, and the chapter on being-toward-death
in particular.[20] The commentary on that text that follows
is intended as a convenient shortcut into the philosophical universe of Heidegger.

Let me begin my account of this specific authentically Heideggerian text with a discussion (a sketch) of
what Heidegger might intend with his crucially important
term *Dasein* (human existence). *Dasein*, we might say, is
the "local" manifestation of Being as a whole—hence all
of us are "particles" of the overall mystery of being, if I
could put it that way. We should live with an ever-present
sense of awe, or at least acute awareness, that we *are* and
that the rest of the world available to us *is*. But we don't.
Instead, we deal with the world and our own presence
in it as if it were the most natural thing in the world for
things to have being. *Wrong*: the natural thing would be
for there to be nothing. In a text entitled "Metaphysics as

History of Being," Heidegger strikingly refers to Being as an "insurrection against nothingness."[21] We live wholly (or at least mainly) in the present, doing our mundane tasks and fulfilling what our mediocre society expects of us in the way of habitual routines. This is what Heidegger calls (234) the "tranquillized everydayness" of inauthentic *Dasein*. No mystery, no awe. Our social existence is prosaic and banal, and for most of us our own experience of life is prosaic and banal. In his book on Schelling, Heidegger calls this "self-stupifying [self-anaesthetizing?] routine" (*sich selbst betäubenden Gewohnheit*),[22] and he clearly regards it as the norm in a democratic culture. Heidegger gives us a particularly powerful statement of his thought in an essay on Heraclitus: Being as Heraclitus experienced it, Being experienced as "lightening," is what has been forgotten in the modern forgetfulness of Being. "We see this lightening only when we station ourselves in the storm of Being. Yet everything today betrays the fact that we bestir ourselves only to drive storms away. We organize all available means for cloud-seeding and storm dispersal in order to have calm in the face of the storm. But this calm is no tranquility. It is only anesthesia; more precisely, the narcotization of anxiety in the face of thinking."[23]

The history of metaphysics ought to convey a sense of how strange and uncanny the world is, and Heidegger thinks that Greek philosophy—before Socrates, Plato, and Aristotle with their rationalism came along—did do this. But the philosophical tradition as shaped by these Greek metaphysical rationalists simply reinforces this dulling of our sense that the presence of a world at all is an unfathomable riddle. The fact that the world exists, the fact that anything exists, is either a miracle or a curse. But whether miracle or curse, we seem to take it utterly for granted, and nothing in our social existence or in our intellectual traditions encourages us to do otherwise; if anything, they merely reinforce whatever it is in our experience of life that dulls or occludes the appreciation of the mysteriousness of being.

But for Heidegger there is a saving grace: death! Death means that we are always standing right on the precipice of utter nothingness. Proper awareness of one's own mortality ought to make this clear to us. Five minutes after writing this sentence, I could suffer a ruptured cerebral aneurism and die on the spot. Immediately, the world in the splendor of its self-disclosure would for me slam shut like a clam! No more Being! No more world! Back to nothingness! As Heidegger rightly says, "What is peculiar to the certainty of death [is] *that it is possible in every moment.* Together with the certainty of death goes the *indefiniteness* of its when" (238). *We stand on the edge of a precipice* and somehow dull or repress our awareness (which at a deeper, more authentic level is never lacking) that that is where we stand, not ever knowing when a little unexpected breeze will come along and tip us into that abyss of being. If only I could be fully alive to this decisive vulnerability to nothingness, Being would start becoming accessible or "meaningful" as the unfathomable riddle that it is. But just as we thoroughly dull ourselves to the "being-ness of being," so we just as thoroughly dull ourselves to the unspeakably radical implications of our standing on the portal of nothingness. Heidegger calls this "the possibility of the measureless impossibility of existence" (242).

Chapter 2

One could easily assume that this couldn't possibly mean anything coherent, but in fact I think we can see fairly well what Heidegger is getting at.

Let me quote a more accessible version of what preoccupies Heidegger that doesn't get so bogged down in Heidegger's ponderous jargon in *Being and Time*. The following is from Samuel Scheffler's provocative book, *Death and the Afterlife*: "Consider this: Every single person now alive will be dead in the not-so-distant future. This fact is universally accepted and is not seen as remarkable, still less as an impending catastrophe. There are no crisis meetings of world leaders to consider what to do about it, no outbreaks of mass hysteria, no outpourings of grief, no demands for action."[24] How do we live at all knowing that death is looming up over all of us? Why aren't we utterly paralyzed by it? There isn't really a good answer to it, and it tells us something interesting about the capacity of human beings to "bracket" what is existentially of supreme ultimacy. I think Heidegger is saying something similar, and it's something that's very much worth saying. In the same vein, Ian McEwan's great novel, *Enduring Love*, also comments tellingly on how little impression death really makes on the mundane course of our lives: "A friend who had been wrongly diagnosed with a terminal illness once told me of the loneliness she had felt as she left the doctor's office. The sympathy of friends simply marked her out with a different fate. She herself had known people who had died, and she knew well enough how life would go on without her. The waters would close over her head, her friends would feel sorrow and then recover, a little wiser, and the unrecorded workdays, parties and dinners would tumble onwards."[25]

Being and Time is intended as an exercise in "fundamental ontology"—that is, an investigation of what it means for beings in general to be, and Heidegger pursues this investigation (there may be other ways of pursuing it, but this is how he pursues it in this particular book) by trying to lay out fundamental structures of human being (*Dasein*: what it means for the kind of beings that *we* are to be).[26] That is, he presents this philosophical inquiry as "structural" or formal; he would dispute the suggestion that the basic categories of his philosophical analysis are "normative" in any sense. But notwithstanding that deliberate self-presentation, one would have to be a little tone-deaf in reading the book not to notice the quite conspicuous "normative resonances" of the book, not excluding his ontological account of death.

Heidegger writes, "The end is imminent for Da-sein" (231). Indeed it is. But he also concedes that "many things can be imminent for Da-sein as being-in-the-world" (232). So why privilege death? I think Heidegger is very clear about this. He says, "It is the most extreme" mode of recognizing what is truly "ownmost" (i.e., of forcing oneself to confront the terror of being absolutely alone in the face of the ultimate realities). "Death is the possibility of the absolute impossibility of Da-sein." It forces upon us "absolute" reflection on the world and how we relate to it. Existence in its totality must be wrestled with in the face of reflection on the unavoidable imminence of the fate whereby the being of the world is, so to speak, *sucked back into nonbeing* (at least for the singular *Dasein* confronting its own death). There is indeed something ontologically "extreme" about knowledge of death as an awareness that the world given to us (as either blessing or curse) will assuredly be *taken back*. The more aware we are of the world's imminent nonbeing, the more intense is our reflection on and ontological relation to its givenness in the first place. This, he says, isn't mere "fear of one's demise" (232); that's too banal. Rather, it's an "Angst" of more metaphysical proportions, or it ought to be if it is to serve Heidegger's function of restoring our attentiveness to "the meaning of being" that we otherwise forget about.

Heidegger's philosophy in *Being and Time* is an ontology of care: human existence (*Dasein*) is as a mode of having things *matter* to us, caring about them or being concerned about them, and relating to a world defined by those existential concerns. Above all, we care about the fact that that world of human concerns will at some point no longer be available to us. We die and our world is no longer there for us. We and our world succumb to nonbeing. So Heidegger's ontology of care is, he would say, *vindicated* by the imperative of caring about whether *we are or we aren't*, about whether *the world is or it isn't* (for that is what is at stake in the death of any singular individual). But the reality is that we *don't* necessarily care about this, or at least not in the way that is privileged by Heidegger's ontological analysis. (Heidegger realizes that this is the case and in fact makes it central to his analysis.) This is where the normative dimension of Heidegger's philosophy becomes more conspicuous. Imagine someone who never for a moment reflected on his or her mortality. Surely, such people exist. In fact, it can't be ruled out (and Heidegger doesn't rule it out) that in a society devoted to a life of complacent bourgeois comforts, a great many people give little or no thought to the meaning of their own mortality. What does Heidegger say about such people? He says that they are *fleeing* from the reality that death will be a retraction of the world that we currently have, and that defines a concernful existence for us. It is "flight from uncanniness" (233).[27] Our own being is uncanny, and people who shy away from full awareness of what death is are thereby fleeing their own being. Being calls out to us (by enforcing awareness that our access to Being is of necessarily finite duration), and we—cowards that we are—run away! So the embrace of uncanniness is a kind of existential *obligation*, and recognizing that our being is essentially being-toward-death is a necessary way of living up to such an obligation. Heidegger writes that inauthentic *Dasein* flees death by "interposing . . . manageable urgencies [as opposed to the 'unmanageable urgency' of our looming mortality!] and possibilities of the everyday matters nearest to us" (239). Well, all of that puts us in recognizably normative territory, even though Heidegger would strongly resist acknowledging the implicit "morality of Angst," if I could call it that.

Heidegger wants to say that he's in the business of ontological analysis, not normative analysis. But there is something insistently normative about his discussion of the "evasion" or "tranquillization" of death:

> The "neighbors" often try to convince the "dying person" that he will escape death and soon return again to the tranquillized everydayness of his world taken care of. This "concern" has the intention of thus "comforting" the "dying person." It wants to bring him back to Da-sein by helping him to veil completely his ownmost nonrelational possibility. Thus, the they makes sure of a *constant tranquillization about death*.[28] But, basically,

this tranquillization is not only for the "dying person,"
but just as much for "those who are comforting him."
(234–235)

We could say that "Being itself" demands a kind of ontological courage. And something at the core of our own
being flees in terror from this ontological challenge:
the challenge of seeing death as it truly is. "Entangled,
everyday being-toward-death is a constant *flight from
death*. Being *toward* the end has the mode of *evading
that end*—reinterpreting it, understanding it inauthenti-
cally, and veiling it" (235). That is, the ultimate standard
is authenticity or inauthenticity, and far from it being part
of the natural order of human existence for individuals to
respond authentically to something utterly constitutive
of their own *Dasein*, ontological "veiling" or "evading"
or "fleeing" is inscribed in the very fabric of human existence. Death gives us an opportunity to embrace genuine
authenticity with respect to the meaning of being, and we
utterly fail that test! The ultimate demand of Being is for
us to relate to it in an untranquilized way, but our "everyday" responses (or nonresponses) to death "fall" into
"constant tranquillization." Death is privileged because it
is "the most extreme possibility of [*Dasein*'s] existence"
(235), and we need precisely confrontation with this "most
extreme possibility" as the condition of an ultimate testing
of whether our relation to being as such is tranquilized or
untranquilized.

Is "tranquilization" an ontological concept or a normative concept? It's normative. Heidegger writes, "The
they does not permit the courage to have Angst about
death" (235). Those who have the "real stuff," the inner

fortitude to live alongside the imminence of nonbeing, possess ontological courage; those who succumb to the society-wide-endorsed "estrangement" from death exhibit ontological cowardice. As for Nietzsche and Weber, the human vocation is to display courage in the face of the starkest realities of human existence. Heidegger's version is that fundamental ontology is for heroes.

Similarly, Heidegger speaks of the human possibility "to exist" as "understanding oneself in the being of [*Dasein's*] being" (242). That is, "existing" is not something that happens spontaneously or naturally or without exertion; on the contrary, "to exist" is demanded of us as a normative challenge. Quite explicitly, we are challenged to turn inert existence, existence that falls short of being seized as a deliberate "project" or commitment, into *authentic* existence (or what we might call ontologically animated existence). Hence, what is presented (misleadingly, I would say) as a strictly "ontological" investigation of structures of human existence as a window into an understanding of structures of being as such in actuality is shot through fairly pervasively with normative challenges and normative judgments.

Heidegger doesn't speak in this context of possible reorganizations of social or cultural life that would be less tranquilized, but surely he believes that such a thing is a meaningful option. Does he think that ancient civilizations like the tragic culture of pre-Socratic Greece were as tranquilized as modern society is? Does "idle talk" exist in the Greek polis, when human beings lived in far closer proximity to "the truth of being"? That seems *extremely* unlikely! When he refers polemically to "the they" (*das Man*), is that a local cultural condition or a universal one?

Surely the former! Yet the abstract "ontological" form in which he lays out this analysis very much suggests that the analysis applies to *all* instantiations of human *Dasein* (i.e., applies equally to all of them). My countersuggestion here is that we see quite clearly from the less formal writings of the 1930s that terms like "tranquilization," "the they," "flight from Angst," and so on are meant to insinuate a robust cultural critique aimed at modern cultural experience in particular. In books like *An Introduction to Metaphysics*, we're no longer involved in the enterprise of fundamental ontology that *Being and Time* aspires to practice, but the rhetoric and polemics *are exactly the same*: modern experience is cowardly and effete, and Heidegger surely has in mind premodern societies that wouldn't be subject to the same polemics (or wouldn't be subject to them to the same extent). In fact, one wonders whether *without* that implicit polemical edge and the normative punch it obviously carries, *Being and Time* would have become quite as famous a book as it actually did become.

Heidegger's core thought in the meditation on death may be expressed as follows: Life as we ordinarily live it is a kind of "sleepwalking." We live in oblivion of what confers depth and drama upon the human condition. "Being" calls out to us to be properly aware that we live on the edge of the abyss of utter nothingness, an abyss any of us could tumble into at any moment,[29] and somehow we live as if that abyss isn't there. Isn't that in itself the most profound existential condemnation of the modern/ liberal/bourgeois mode of life? Don't we require a cultural revolution of epic proportions in order to shake us out of this condition of existential sleepwalking? In the same vein, Heidegger writes, "The lives of men began to slide into a world which lacked that depth from out of which the essential always comes to man."[30] Richard Rorty, at the end of his essay "On Heidegger's Nazism," makes the not unreasonable point that in order to profit from Heidegger in ways that don't involve various kinds of political and cultural pathology, one must "stop yearning for depth."[31] Rorty is probably right that this fixation on depth contributes crucially to why things go fundamentally off the rails with Heidegger. The problem is that Heidegger minus the yearning for depth would no longer be Heidegger!

Of course, I'm not saying that one *shouldn't* think about death as a portal to deeper reflection about the uncanniness of human existence and of being in general. What I'm objecting to, I guess, is the underhandedness of Heidegger's rhetoric. On the one hand, he claims to be engaging in an analysis of structural universals that are part and parcel of the human condition; on the other hand, he sneaks in surreptitious polemics contrived for the purpose of getting us to yearn for some more ancient culture and politics supposedly more primordial than the shallow culture and politics we currently have. One could say that Nietzsche, Freud, Weber, and Heidegger are all committed to the following normative principle: we are bound by an existential obligation to live lives that are untranquilized. Two of these thinkers affirm and two of them deny that it follows from this principle that we must do everything in our power to repudiate liberal modernity from top to bottom.

There is only one philosopher directly quoted within the text of the "being-toward-death" chapter. Who is that? Of course! It's Nietzsche—a quotation from the "On Free Death" section of the first part of *Thus Spoke Zarathustra*

(244).[32] That is no accident. It helps flag for us the fact that Heidegger's purpose is to articulate an "ontological task" (240) that is as bracing and that rises to the same existential heights as Nietzsche's root-and-branch questioning of modernity's (limp) horizon of life. That is true not only of early Heidegger but also of more mature Heidegger, as we'll see in the next section.

Post-Nazi Heidegger: *Letter on Humanism*

> Who has not felt superior to humanism? It is the cheapest target of all: Humanism is sentimental, flabby, bourgeois, hypocritical, complacent, middlebrow, liberal, sanctimonious, constricting and often an alibi for power. The abusers of humanism, of course, are guilty of none of those sins. From Heidegger to Althusser, they come as emancipators. I think we should emancipate ourselves from their emancipations.
>
> —Leon Wieseltier[33]

The *Letter on Humanism*, read carefully, is a disturbing text. And as with many of Heidegger's important works, the more one exerts oneself to draw a political philosophy out of it, the more disturbing it gets.

As is well known, the main narrative of the *Letter* concerns a far-reaching critique of the history of Western metaphysics: "Thinking is the thinking of Being."[34] Customarily, we would presume that thinking means thinking about X or Y or Z. But, Heidegger insists, that is not real thinking. Real authentic thinking is the pondering of the *being* of X or Y or Z. That is, all real thinking is directed toward the mystery of being whereby X or Y or Z *are*, and thinking concerned with X, Y, or Z that *abstracts* from this mystery or uncanniness of being is condemned as shallow: "ontic" (oriented to given beings) rather than "ontological" (oriented to the unfathomable "Being" that gives or discloses or renders available these beings). The history of philosophy as we have known it since Plato contributes to this shallowness, and insofar as we are now in the pervasive grip of a whole civilization that is shallow through and through, we ultimately have the traditions of Western philosophy to blame for this foreclosed access to the profundity or primordiality of Being. As Heidegger puts it, "Even such names as 'logic,' 'ethics,' and 'physics' begin to flourish only when original thinking comes to an end. During the time of their greatness, the Greeks thought without such headings. They did not even call thinking 'philosophy'" (219–220; cf. 256). These are characteristic Heideggerian tropes, and they display recognizable Nietzschean provenance.

Apart from Nietzsche and Heidegger, it would be a universal view that the moment of greatness of ancient Greek philosophy ran from Socrates to Aristotle via Plato. Nietzsche was the first to declare that the true grandeur of ancient philosophy predated Socrates, and Heidegger offers his own ambitious version of that revisionist thesis of Nietzsche's. The fact that Aristotle's philosophy can be divided into "logic" and "ethics" and "physics" already shows that authentically ontological thinking has been reduced to a lower level, a merely "ontic" level (investigation of X or Y or Z, whatever X, Y, or Z happen to be). That "lowering" or corruption from the ontological level to the ontic level is ultimately the doing of Plato, the thinker who committed the "original sin" of Western thought. Put otherwise, thinking in its heroic phase becomes merely prosaic and commonplace. Heidegger is following Nietzsche's lead in adopting this kind of rhetoric. Thinkers come in two basic varieties: the heroic thinkers who "think Being"; and the banal thinkers who merely think beings (X or Y or Z). Our whole civilization is banal because it has taken its bearings from thinkers of the second variety rather than those of the first. But thanks to Heidegger, it is not too late to reverse course. We can resume where Heraclitus and Parmenides left off and bypass the long detour from Plato to the nineteenth century. Nietzsche, unknowingly (on Heidegger's account), was part of or an expression of the long, failed metaphysical detour taken by Western thinking, but Heidegger can restore it to the true path.

This is a grand mythology, with noble heroes and low villains (not dissimilar to Nietzsche's noble heroes and low villains). The immediate target of the *Letter* is Jean-Paul Sartre. (The letter to Jean Beaufret on which the text is based was written in 1946, the same year that Sartre published his famous lecture, "Existentialism is a Humanism.") Sartre takes himself to stand outside or beyond the metaphysical tradition, which he assumes has reached its end. This is superficially similar to Heidegger's claim, but Sartre appeals to the idea of human subjectivity as a self-grounding manifestation of freedom, action, and *l'engagement* ("commitment"). For Heidegger, appeal to subjectivity is still very much *part of* the metaphysical tradition originating with Plato and fails to penetrate to the deeper mode of thinking oriented to Being that gets corrupted into the more shallow division of the world into mere subjects and mere objects. To distinguish between subjects and objects is already to implicate oneself in the kind of "ontic" relationship to the world that betrays philosophy's having cut itself off from Being in its profundity and mystery. Sartre is as banal as Descartes, and Descartes is as banal as Aristotle. They all fail the test of truly *heroic* thinking focused on Being as an abyss that tests our existential mettle to the limit. "Existentialism" presents itself as heroic, face to face with death, the absurd, and the possibility of the meaninglessness of existence, but all of this looks pretty paltry compared with the world-shattering experience of "thinking" to which Heidegger thinks the Greeks rose "during the time of their greatness" and which he alone (heralded by Nietzsche and Nietzsche's failure to liberate himself fully from metaphysics) is capable of resuming.

As Heidegger says on p. 221, "philosophy" as such already represents a degeneration from the ontological domain to the ontic domain. Philosophy as a discipline is divided into various "isms," one of which is "existentialism." "The thinking that is to come," Heidegger writes at the end of the text, "is no longer philosophy, because it thinks more originally than metaphysics—a name identical to philosophy" (265). Nietzsche and Sartre are part of the philosophical tradition, and hence they too are part of the essential problem—namely, being implicated in the metaphysical tradition that alienates us from "the nearness of Being" (242). They, no less than all other participants in the philosophical tradition, founder with respect to the truly ontological achievement of authentic thinking in the company of Being. They are metaphysicians who have duped themselves into believing themselves liberated from metaphysics. (Jacques Derrida later deploys the same kind of rhetorical trick against Heidegger himself!)

It is easy enough to draw from Heidegger a picture of life in liberal-egalitarian modernity as governed by alienation from, or oblivion in relation to, the meaning of what it means to be. Yet what concretely is to be associated with the notion of "nearness to Being"? Here Heidegger supplies little that is tangible. This is what some have called Heidegger's "pseudo-concreteness,"[35] though it isn't impossible to extrapolate from certain Heideggerian gestures. The asymmetry between the concreteness of what Heidegger is attacking and the abstraction or vagueness with respect to what he is celebrating is obviously a problem. Still, we can locate some texts within the *Letter on Humanism* that give us a somewhat clearer indication of what Heidegger hopes for by way of a new dispensation—namely, one that will deliver the desired nearness to Being. In particular, starting on p. 224, Heidegger traces a history of humanism, beginning with the Hellenistic Greeks, via the Romans, via the Renaissance,[36] and then arriving at the German "humanism of the eighteenth century [borne] by Winckelmann, Goethe, and Schiller" (225). Yet there's a countertradition, and Heidegger clearly aligns himself with this countertradition: "Hölderlin does not belong to 'humanism,' precisely because he thought the destiny of man's essence in a more original [*anfänglicher*: more originary? more primordial?] way than 'humanism' could" (ibid.; cf. 241–243).[37] Classical humanists like Goethe and Schiller are less "original," presumably because they build on Renaissance conceptions, which in turn are built on Roman conceptions, and so on, whereas Hölderlin circumvents those spiritually depleted traditions and connects directly with the *real* origin—Being itself (as does Heidegger!). As Heidegger develops his conception of the distinction on pp. 225–226, it's clear that in his view there are the shallow humanisms, going all the way back to the Greeks, that fail to "ask about the truth of Being" because they presume "metaphysical" predeterminations of the essence of the human being, and on the other side, the more primordial humanism associated with Hölderlin—more primordial because it does orient its questioning concerning the essence of the human being to the deeper questioning directed toward the truth of Being: the disclosure of a genuinely historical world in its uncanniness[38] and unfathomableness. (Note Heidegger's reference on p. 243 to the "mere" cosmopolitanism [*das bloße Weltbürgertum*] of Goethe—a text to which we'll return.)

How does Heidegger show that the tradition of "metaphysical humanism" is shallow relative to the non-metaphysical humanism or antihumanism he celebrates? His first argument is telling. The metaphysical tradition posits the human essence as *animal rationale*. Heidegger (226) claims that *Being and Time* succeeded in excavating "the essential provenance of metaphysics," thereby allowing those schooled by Heidegger to grasp that the metaphysical determination of man as rational animal falls short of being able to think the difference between beings and Being and thereby doesn't plumb the authentic depths of the human essence. The idea of man as rational animal (the metaphysical definition of man par excellence) is lacking in primordiality, in depth, because it fails to attend thinkingly to Being as the origin, the dwelling-place, of *Dasein*, the potential "shepherd" of Being (234).

The metaphysical tendency to attribute "soul," "reason," or "personality" to the human animal counts for Heidegger as an "insufficient definition of man's essence" (229). *Dasein* captures the essence of the human because it highlights the human vocation to be aware of itself as the *Da* (the "there") of Being (*Sein*): that is, the site of "the clearing of Being," the place where Being discloses itself in its character as fate or destiny (ibid.).

In Heidegger's view, the metaphysical tradition wrongly conceives Being to be merely a common property that runs through all beings and that can be apprehended by the light of reason, and this misconception of Being ultimately has pervasively catastrophic consequences for history, culture, and politics. Heidegger's rhetoric of "metaphysics" as the supreme villain responsible for everything that isn't right with the world has obviously been an astonishingly effective and influential rhetoric. Derrida, for instance—and postmodernism more broadly—is unthinkable without that rhetoric. But the rhetoric doesn't really tell us anything until we have a more definite conception of the non-metaphysical or postmetaphysical approach to the world that will supplant the metaphysics that has stretched from Plato to the nineteenth century. So what fills that empty box in Heidegger's thought, as articulated in the *Letter on Humanism* as an exemplary Heideggerian text?

Heidegger, starting on p. 241, returns to the question of Hölderlin over against the totality of the rest of Western thought, more or less.[39] The issue here is the possibility of experiencing a sense of "homeland" (*Heimat*), versus "the homelessness [*Heimatlosigkeit*] of contemporary man."[40] Heidegger wants to say that metaphysical conceptions of the human animal, whether in terms of reason or soul or personality, prove themselves to be "insufficient definitions of man's essence" precisely because they issue ultimately in "the homelessness of contemporary man." Redirecting thought concerning what it is to be human from, say, the idea of the rational animal to man as the *Da* of Being, or as the shepherd of the mystery of Being, or as the place where the clearing of Being "happens"— all of which are alternative formulations of, or metaphors for, the same basic conception—will, if successful, restore "home" or "dwelling" to what is homeless. Nietzsche, Heidegger says, "experienced this homelessness" (241) but didn't fix the problem because he offered merely a "reversal" (= inversion) of the metaphysical mode of thinking rather than broke out of it. Nietzsche perceived the problem but couldn't solve it. Why does Heidegger think that Nietzsche had a unique experience of the "homelessness" of modernity? This is a crucial question for the interpretation of the *Letter on Humanism*. My own view is that what Heidegger is here calling homelessness represents his attempt to translate into his own terms what we in chapter 1 characterized as Nietzsche's critique of "horizonlessness." For both of them, the open-horizoned universalism of modernity, as well as modern humanity's tendency to think according to a day-to-day or week-to-week rather than century-to-century time frame, makes it impossible for human cultures to be genuine cultures. Nietzsche's solution is for ruling elites of the future to will into existence binding cultural horizons that are as remote from modernity as they can possibly be. Heidegger's solution is to await a new experience of attunement to Being that will be at the same time the recovery of a genuine experience of rootedness. This in turn draws Heidegger into a kind of "blood and soil" thinking that would have been anathema to Nietzsche.

With respect to Heidegger's ambition to identify a solution to the problem of modern homelessness that he thinks eluded Nietzsche, Heidegger's privileging of Hölderlin over against the so-called metaphysical tradition again appears pivotal. Hölderlin beckons the Germans to connect with the essence of Germanness and to do so not for prosaically "patriotic" or "nationalistic" purposes but rather in order to achieve "belongingness to the destiny of the West." And not merely the West but "world-historically out of nearness to the source" (241). One needs to acquire a "homeland" in order to become fatefully world-historical; and one needs to become fatefully world-historical in order to overcome "the homelessness of contemporary man." What is at stake in the poetry of Hölderlin is not merely proper rootedness in the essence of being German but in fact overcoming of alienation from Being, because "homelessness . . . consists in the abandonment of Being by beings. Homelessness is the symptom of oblivion of Being" (242). Or rather, rootedness in the homeland and healing of the alienation from Being *are one and the same thing*.[41] I think one starts to get the picture. The least rude thing one can say here is that it shows a lot of chutzpah on the part of Heidegger to talk about German Romantic poetry and nationalism as a guiding vehicle for "fatefulness," "world-historicalness," "the destiny of the West," and recollection of Being itself a mere eighteen months after German nationalism had left the world in ruins!

The key passage comes on pp. 242–243: "The world-historical thinking of Hölderlin [is] essentially more primordial and thus more significant for the future than the mere cosmopolitanism of Goethe." This hostile reference to Goethe is a reminder of Heidegger's famous 1929 Davos debate with Ernst Cassirer, who presented himself as a representative of precisely the humanism of Goethe. Geoff Waite has claimed that Cassirer specifically cited Goethe because he was "likely aware that Heidegger loathed Goethe."[42] Here, at any rate, that loathing seems to be made explicit. "Hölderlin's relation to Greek civilization is something essentially other than humanism," implying that Goethe as a classic expression of mainstream Western culture derives ultimately from the shallow rationalism/ universalism of Socrates and Plato, whereas Hölderlin connects to something far deeper and more authentic in the Greek experience of Being. "*When confronted with death*, . . . those young Germans who knew about Hölderlin lived and thought something other than what the public held to be the typical German attitude" (243; my italics). Heidegger doesn't say what constitutes "the typical German attitude" or precisely what confrontation with death draws these young Germans into a more primordial expression of life and thought. But he does offer a very clear gesture back toward the "being-toward-death" chapter of *Being and Time* and hints strongly that dying gloriously for the German homeland (with Hölderlin in mind!) puts one in the vicinity of the kind of authentic existence that *Being and Time* is intended to valorize. The underlying message seems clear. Hölderlin-inspired German nationalism is "rooted" and hence near to Being. All alternatives to that kind of romantically charged-up/ reactionary German nationalism are "homeless" and hence remote from Being. Recall again that Heidegger

was writing this in *1946*, when it was blindingly obvious to everyone (including the Germans) that hero-
ically inflected German nationalism had destroyed
Europe and very nearly reduced civilization to universal
barbarism.

To be sure, there are passages in the *Letter* (241 and
244) where Heidegger makes noises intended to put dis-
tance between a conventional nationalism aimed at mere
power and supremacy for Germany, and his supposedly
more "spiritual," more metaphysical variety of German
nationalism.[43] I don't take these disclaimers very seriously. By contrast to conventional nationalism, which
seeks merely to exalt the German *Volk* in relation to other
nations, Heidegger's nationalism is aimed at plugging the
Volk into the destiny of Being in its unfathomable depth
and uncanniness. For sure, it is a *spookier* nationalism (or
at least one enveloped in a more mystical rhetoric). Still, as
we saw with the text celebrating the young Germans "confronting death" in communion with Hölderlin's poetry,
there are definite points of intersection between his version and the version that prompted a bid for the dictato-
rial enslavement of Europe, leading to World War II and
the Holocaust. In any case, what I draw from all this is that
Heidegger's purpose is to elevate the "homeland" even
higher than it is elevated by ordinary nationalism. After
all, the *Volk* is far more heroic ("metaphysically" or ontologically heroic) if it serves as the guardian of Being than
if it is merely in the service of the glory of Germany.

The philosophically more important point is this: for
Heidegger, the history of metaphysics is shallow because it
seduces us into thinking that we stand on solid and com-
prehensible ground. Privileging our identity as rational

beings is a key part of this error since it reinforces our confidence that we can know and master the world and hence rest content with mere commerce with beings. The truth of Being, by contrast, means that what we "stand" on is pure groundlessness: the abysmal mystery of Being as the "ungrounded ground" of *Dasein*. Heidegger doesn't use the language of *Übermenschen*, but it seems clear that the whole pathos of Heidegger's writings rests on the suggestion that if we really faced up to the truth of Being and proved ourselves equal to it, we would vindicate ourselves as a new kind of *Übermenschen*: oriented not to the bathos of life in a fully rationalized and banalized modernity but to the higher mysteries and the sublime destiny of nearness to Being. (I say that Heidegger avoids talk of *Übermenschen*, but there is one significant Heideggerian text in which he tellingly fuses Nietzsche's idea of the *Übermensch* with his own idea of the disclosure of Being: "'Overman' is the man who grounds Being anew—in the rigor of knowledge and in the grand style of creation."[44])

As is also the case with the early text treated in the previous section, the purpose of Heidegger's rhetoric is to play up the sense of terror and cosmic loneliness in a world suspended over the abyss of the unplumbable event or "happening" of Being bringing forth beings, as well as the underlying natural but typically repressed Angst concerning the groundlessness of it all. And yet the world gets on with its tedious, commonplace business as if everything were entirely solid and under rational control. How could we be so oblivious to the fact of the pure inexplicable givenness of the world?

But here's my challenge: it's fine for Heidegger to make these claims. But on what basis can he persuade us that he isn't just pulling (imaginary) rabbits out of hats? Do we simply take it on his singular authority that "Being" intends a special destiny for *Dasein* and that we have to embrace a kind of heroism of "ecstatic" existence in order to fulfill that destiny? What if it's all just a concoction of his own manic philosophical imagination? (Obviously I'm not the first reader of Heidegger to raise this sort of challenge.) Why would "Being" select out one particular nation for this privileged destiny or select "*Dasein*" (i.e., one particular species on a very minuscule and obscure planet), for that matter? Of course, the world religions have always been in the business of making these kinds of far-fetched claims, and with just as little basis beyond the arbitrary authority of charismatic prophets and preachers. Like Nietzsche, Heidegger seems to have reinvented the idea of what philosophy should be in a way that renders it a kind of hybrid of, or intermediate possibility between, theory and (atheistic) religion. This is expressed in the fact that both of them exhibit a conspicuous lack of hesitation or reserve in deploying a grandly prophetic tone in their writings—a grandly prophetic tone that, conveniently enough, is marvelously effective in attracting readers and disciples. (Needless to say, the worry about false prophets that we quoted from Stanley Rosen at the head of this chapter applies with equal force to both of them.)

The ultimate answer to the question of whether Heidegger's philosophy is or isn't a form of humanism is presented as a response to Sartre's suggestion that in the wake of the death of God, we are "in a situation where there are only human beings" (237). Heidegger strenuously denies this. There is no God, but there are human beings and there is fateful and unfathomable Being—the "clearing" that brings forth human beings, that brings forth both nature and history. Heidegger's stunning feat here, and it should not be minimized, is to have hit upon a way of continuing to conceive of the world, and human beings within it, as a *gift* even if it is not the gift of a Creator-God. According to Heidegger, this gift-like character of the world is inscribed in the German idiom, *es gibt* (there is = it gives). "This '*es gibt*' rules as a destiny of Being. Its history comes to language in the words of essential thinkers. Therefore the thinking that thinks into the truth of Being is, as thinking, historical" (238). Being = destiny. This is Heidegger's historicism: What happens historically is not simply a function of human agency but the "giving" that emanates from what constitutes the *es* that is referred to in *es gibt*. On p. 255, Heidegger writes, "Being . . . has made itself known in the present moment of world history by the uprooting of all beings." That is, we live in a technological age not because millions of human beings have opted, rightly or wrongly, for the possibilities of life that modern technology makes available to them, but because this is the destiny that "Being" has chosen for us. As Heidegger puts it on p. 240, the luminous manifestation of the *Da* "is the dispensation of Being itself." It follows from this that human existence as we live it historically (*Dasein*) is not something created or fashioned ultimately by human beings; it is given to us, which is something we appreciate if and only if we attend more to the *es gibt* than we attend to ourselves as mere beings. It also follows from this fundamental repudiation of subjectivism (and hence "humanism" as a mode of subjectivism) that Sartre is in a crucial sense more the heir of Nietzsche than Heidegger is. This departure from Nietzsche (formulated as Nietzsche being still a metaphysical thinker and Heidegger being a decisively postmetaphysical thinker) is at the core of Heidegger's self-understanding or philosophical identity.

Hans-Georg Gadamer, the most consequential of Heidegger's disciples, once said in an interview that "when [Heidegger] first started coming out with his mysterious allusions to the return of the gods, we were really shocked."[45] We get just this kind of talk on p. 242. Gadamer says that he got in touch with Heidegger and Heidegger reassured him that such talk was not to be taken too literally. Fine. Yet if Heidegger doesn't literally expect an epiphany of awaited gods, what's the function of this kind of talk? (Another question: If Heidegger says to Gadamer that we shouldn't take too literally his talk of "the return of the gods," why should we take any more literally the talk of "nearness to Being," etc.?)

Heidegger's rhetoric is implicitly Nietzschean. We are enveloped in a universal "night" of utter oblivion of Being; we await a Nietzschean "dawn of day" when Being decides to give us the means to dwell once again in nearness to Being. We are homeless; we await a return to our *Heimat*. We live a Being-granted "destiny" or we live utterly alienated from historicity. Like Nietzsche, it's either "last man" or *Übermensch*; *there is no middle ground*. Hence we have to await the epiphany, the return of the gods, the return from homelessness to authentic dwelling, that will (in the words of the *Der Spiegel* interview) "save us." Being gives us new gods or we are consigned to complete forsakenness; Being gives us poets and thinkers who restore our sense of rootedness or we are utterly homeless; Being gives us destiny or we are left in a state of limitless alienation. (Heidegger approves of Marx's talk of wholesale alienation [243].) It was misguided eschatological thinking of this sort that led Heidegger in 1933 to think that he was in the vanguard of a "revolution" that would usher in a whole new dispensation for Germany and for the world under Germany's leadership. But thirteen years later, the basic structure of his thinking is no different. One feels compelled to say that here is a man who experienced political events without really experiencing them.

Someone might object: What's the point of submitting a text that's fundamentally philosophical—that's preoccupied by the history of metaphysics, for instance—to a critique that's so directly political? As should be clear by now, I don't buy this argument. For me, what is in question here is the *political philosophy* of the *Letter on Humanism*. That the philosophy includes a political philosophy is simply unavoidable; a philosopher as ambitious as Heidegger is virtually guaranteed to have a political philosophy. And one obviously can't have a political philosophy that's nonpolitical. So the politics of the *Letter on Humanism* (albeit a politics that is subtle or perhaps somewhat duplicitous) is fair game.[46]

Heidegger concludes the *Letter* with a lavish display of *humility*: we must lower our expectations of philosophy. The thinker is like the humble peasant, descending "to the poverty of [thinking's] provisional essence" (265). The "inconspicuous furrows in language" laid by the thinker are "more inconspicuous than the furrows that the farmer, slow of step, draws through the field." The humble peasant communes with the mystery of Being by living in "nearness" to Being, and the humble thinker does the same. This pastoral imagery harks back to the formulations offered earlier in the *Letter* according to which the thinker is merely the shepherd of Being, not the lord of beings (234 and 245). "The essential poverty of the shepherd" (245) is a gain and not a loss since the relinquishing of mastery over beings is a condition of attaining to the truth of Being. That stance of the peasant-like humility of the postmetaphysical, postphilosophical "thinker" is largely a theatrical pose on the part of Heidegger: a rhetoric—one that actually exalts him above all previous contributors to the philosophical tradition! There's a dialectic of hubris and humility throughout this text, and it's not obvious whether the humility exceeds the hubris or the hubris exceeds the humility. Clearly, I lean toward the latter interpretation.

Why should we be skeptical of Heidegger's professions of peasant-like humility? Heidegger's closing theme is that philosophy needs a new appreciation of the stringency of its limits in the world of praxis. True! But he is dissembling when he presents himself as the exemplar of the earnestly desired humility of the thinker. On p. 258 he writes that ethics rightly construed "ponders the abode of man"; "that thinking which thinks the truth of Being as the primordial element of man . . . is in itself the original ethics." That is, Heraclitus—because of his direct communing with the truth of Being—is suitably plugged into the Greek "ethos" (Sophocles is as well) and hence offers a more "primordial" ethics than that offered by Aristotle or any other representative of the history of moral philosophy. And who is Heraclitus's successor in practicing this more primordial form of "ethics"? Heidegger. Hence I'd suggest that we take Heidegger's appeals to the humility of the thinker (matching "the essential poverty of the shepherd") with a very large grain of salt.

We get a similar formulation in Heidegger's *An Intro-duction to Metaphysics*: ethos as "the shaping of man's historical being" was "under the influence of morality . . . later degraded to the ethical."[47] That is, ethos reaches to the ontological depths of our existence because it is in direct communion with a historical revelation/bodying-forth of Being, relative to which "the ethical," as a mere appreciation of virtues and vices, is ontologically "degraded." Or, to put it in Nietzschean terms, the experience of Being is beyond good and evil. Any reader of Heidegger who doesn't find this a little disturbing perhaps needs to think harder about what he is saying in this and related texts.

I think Heidegger would say (in fact, it's implicit throughout his writings) that the very fact that a city like Los Angeles exists proves that the history of the West has culminated in our being profoundly alienated from historicity, alienated from the truth of Being, and alienated from the tragic depth of human existence qua *Dasein*.[48] (I actually composed this sentence while I was in an airplane looking down on LA. The thought suddenly came to me: What would Heidegger think of all this? As soon as one poses that question, it's pretty obvious that if LA isn't the very epitome of *Seinsvergessenheit* [forgetfulness of Being], then nothing is—just as the Black Forest is, in a Heideggerian view, the closest we can come to being capable of a genuine recollection or appropriation of the truth of Being.) By contrast to the inauthentic and deracinated existence available in a modern urban metropolis, Being and historicity are fully present in Heidegger's own cabin in the Black Forest just as they were present in the temples of ancient Greece, put into a "primordial saying" by Heraclitus and Sophocles. This, I suspect, is what is meant by *language as the house of Being* (probably the *Letter*'s most famous line): one can genuinely "dwell" in the animating presence of Being when Ur-poets and Ur-thinkers find the words that summon Being out of its absence or silence. In order for Being and "the gods" to return, one would have to somehow conjure away modernity in its totality and supplant it with a whole new civilization founded on the *ethos* experienced by Heraclitus and captured in his *pre*metaphysical thinking or the *ethos* experienced by Heidegger in his ski hut and captured in his *post*metaphysical thinking. Are Heidegger's followers (who are content to parrot his jargon and appear unconcerned by the lack of content of his endlessly repeated formulas) aware that this is what he's saying?[49] And if so, are they prepared to endorse this approach to life as superior to the alternatives?

Heidegger's basic idea, it seems, is that peasants, soldiers, and Romantic poets have a capacity for "communing with Being" that ordinary intellectuals and the educated middle class will never have. The history of the West is a process rendering our experience of the mystery of existence progressively more and more superficial, and "modernity" is the culmination (or the final nadir) of this process. Hence modernity has to be destroyed, and the sooner the better. Consider Leo Strauss's telling encapsulation of what those under the immediate spell of Heidegger took the project to be: "Enthusiastic pupils of Heidegger said that *Martin* Heidegger marks the end of the epoch which was opened by another Martin, Martin Luther."[50] In other words, in order to imagine what habitation of a genuinely Heideggerian ethical-political universe would comprise, we would need to begin imagining what life would be like if human beings had never experienced the democratizing cultural revolutions associated with the Reformation and the Enlightenment, if urbanization and industrialization had never happened, and if Christian monotheism had never displaced the gods of the pagan world. And as for the privileging of Heraclitus and Sophocles, it's eye-opening and starkly sobering to see how images of ancient Greece figure in the iconography of the contemporary far right. Just look at some ultraright websites! I can more or less guarantee that it will have a strong effect on how one thereafter responds to Heideggerian (and Nietzschean) Hellenophile rhetoric. It's easy to be drawn to the abstract language of "Being" as long as it's serving to discredit those aspects of modernity that we dislike, but are any of us really prepared to entertain the possibility of the comprehensive cancelling-out of modernity to which Heidegger in his radicalism seems committed? And are we taking Heidegger seriously if we fail to think through exactly what this radicalism signifies?

Heidegger's Shell Game

For the attentive reader of Heidegger's work, nothing is more disturbing than the evident politically and strategically motivated doctoring of texts in Heidegger's postwar publications.[51] There are two versions of Heidegger's book on Schelling. The first was published in 1971; the second was published in 1988 as part of his *Collected Works*. In the part of the book corresponding to pp. 22–23 of the Joan Stambaugh translation,[52] Heidegger inserts several paragraphs offering a discussion of Nietzsche's views concerning nihilism. A long sentence at the end of one of these paragraphs that appeared in the original lectures was omitted from the 1971 version[53] (and hence is absent from the Stambaugh translation) but was reinstated in the 1988 version.[54] Here is my translation of the text that was suppressed and then later reinstated: "As is well known, both of the two men in Europe who have, in the political-national fashioning of their respective Volks, inaugurated counter-movements [*Gegenbewegungen*] to nihilism, namely Mussolini and Hitler, were in turn, each in their own way, essentially determined by Nietzsche; still, this was so without Nietzsche's authentic metaphysical domain having properly come into its own." This originates in a lecture course given in the summer of 1936.[55] The following winter (1936–37), Heidegger gave the first set of his lectures on Nietzsche. Here too there was a damning text that was omitted from the edition of 1961 yet reinstated in the 1985 edition of the *Collected Works*:[56] "Europe still wants to cling to 'democracy' and does not want to see that this would constitute its historical death. For democracy is, as Nietzsche clearly saw, only a degenerate form [*eine Abart*] of nihilism." The two texts are complementary: Democracy = nihilism. Nietzsche is the thinker who understood this most clearly. Mussolini and Hitler were the two political figures who sought to learn what Nietzsche had to teach and to apply countermeasures in practice (even if they fell short of Heidegger's own deeper understanding of the metaphysical significance of Nietzsche). Contemporary Europe offers three concrete alternatives: liberalism, communism, and fascism. The first two stand for "leveling" and the "historical demise" of Europe; the third stands for grandeur and rebirth. These affirmations are not to be found in political speeches delivered by Heidegger in 1933 functioning as a quasi-official of the regime; they are delivered in academic lectures on metaphysical topics three to four years later.

It seems apparent that there is a pattern here. The *Collected Works* was supervised by Heidegger's son, and large decisions about the edition were, it seems, dictated by Heidegger himself. Reinstatement of these texts, presumably, was deliberate. Why would Heidegger be willing to sanction the publication of texts (published posthumously in 1985 and 1988) that he self-consciously repressed (for obvious reasons) in 1961 and 1971 respectively? For what it's worth, here's a quick statement of my own theory. On Heidegger's view one needs to think in centuries.[57] He assumed that people would be reading him for centuries (just as one continues to read Aristotle or Hegel). The twentieth century was a lost cause. No point in generating needless hostility to his books, so one should make local, short-term concessions to a benighted age. But eventually people would forget Mussolini and Hitler and remember Heidegger. Three hundred years from now, people would see that philosophically, Heidegger was right, even if he made some tactical mistakes in the '30s. (Over the span of centuries, who would care what happened in the 1930s?) Gadamer once said (in the context of defending Heidegger!) that Heidegger, "true visionary" that he was, was so preoccupied by modernity's forgetfulness of Being that even the Nazi genocide "appeared to him as something minimal compared to the future that awaits us."[58] That seems correct. For Heidegger, the extermination of European Jewry was "small change" compared with what modernity is doing to the experience of Being.

So if what counts is the struggle against modernity spread over centuries, what is needed is a definitive version of Heidegger's views in their historical totality. Hence the doctoring of his texts in 1961 and 1971 had to be undone or *un*doctored—that is, annulled. (The same interpretation can presumably be applied to the decision to publish the *Black Notebooks*.) The Gesamtausgabe is advertised as being an "edition of the last hand," which means that what counts is the final version as authorized definitively by Heidegger. What the reinstatement of earlier deletions (the annulling of those deletions) tells us is that this final version displays a defiantly unrepentant Heidegger, with his "private National Socialism"[59] (his National Socialism that was superior to Hitler's) intact.

Two Anecdotes

The question of how to assess Heidegger philosophically was at the heart of the intellectual relationship between two of the leading German theorists of the last half-century: Jürgen Habermas and Hans-Georg Gadamer. I've been doing theory since the 1970s, hence I've had the good fortune to encounter these two eminent philosophers, both of whom importantly influenced my own career as a political theorist. In February of 1979, I attended a talk in Oxford by Habermas. He made some disparaging remarks about Gadamer, so I put up my hand and asked a question, pointing out a whole series of intellectual commonalities between Habermas and Gadamer. Habermas looked very annoyed and paused with deliberate dramatic effect to light a cigar. He responded with a question:

"What are you, an American?" "No, a Canadian." "OK, a Canadian. Well, you don't understand the German context." End of reply. Charles Taylor and Richard Bernstein were in the room. I know that Taylor at least was shocked by this response. Here was Habermas, the great champion of universalistic dialogue, rejecting my right even to ask the question on grounds of bare nationality. As is perfectly clear in retrospect, he was flagging Heidegger, and Gadamer's intellectual fidelity to Heidegger, without mentioning Heidegger's name.[60]

Five years later I found myself having dinner with the eighty-four-year-old Gadamer at Chez Piggy's in Kingston, Ontario. (He ordered steak tartare, so I followed the master and ordered the same.) I put the same question in reverse—that is, I asked Gadamer what was his view of Habermas. His response too was shocking. As I best recollect his words, they were as follows: "Habermas is not really a philosopher, he's more like a sociologist. He's incapable of taking Heidegger seriously, and that by itself proves he's no philosopher." If I remember correctly, he also complained that Habermas "politicizes everything." It's obviously telling that Heidegger figured crucially in both responses. At the time, and for many years thereafter, I sided with Gadamer. To align Gadamer with reactionary German conservatism, as Habermas implicitly did, seemed grossly unfair to Gadamer; and on the other side, Gadamer seemed right to say that an incapacity to recognize the greatness of Heidegger qua philosopher was to the intellectual discredit of Habermas. However, I have over the last couple of years, for reasons sketched in this book, swung over to leaning much more on the side of Habermas.

Chapter 2

Philosophy as such is a universalistic enterprise. As Plato rightly suggested at the very outset, philosophy is the aspired-to exit from particular caves and their parochial opinions. Nietzsche and Heidegger, by attacking the history of Western rationalism, simultaneously undermine the universalism of philosophy. Although I was shocked by Habermas's response at the time, I now see that he was probably right to point out that "the German context" was more relevant to Heidegger's efforts as a philosopher than I then appreciated and therefore right too in suggesting that this context and his ostensibly incriminating implication in it does indeed impugn Heidegger as an exemplar of the universalistic calling that is philosophy.[61]

Nietzsche and Heidegger; Freud and Weber

There's a celebrated dictum of the elderly Heidegger reported by Gadamer: "Nietzsche ruined me."[62] What could Heidegger have meant by that? Here's a bit of speculation on my part about what it *could have* meant. Heidegger was persuaded by Nietzsche's critique of the decadence and "homelessness" or rootlessness of liberal modernity (its "nihilism"). In the course of the 1920s and early '30s, he came to the view that the Nazi version of destiny, spirit, and power represented *antidecadence*—that is, the remedy for liberal/modern spiritlessness. However, in the late '30s and early '40s, Heidegger started to perceive German fascism not as an essential antidote to modernity but as *part of* modernity's alienation from some deeper ontological reality and its destruction of the human essence. In its essence, Nazism (Heidegger had at some point realized) did not stand *outside* the boundaries of modernity conceived as the negation of the truth of Being but rather *inside* those boundaries. Liberating himself from Nazism thus required the monumental effort of liberating himself from Nietzsche—hence the famous "confrontation" (*Auseinandersetzung*) with Nietzsche requiring a truly epic interpretation of Nietzsche as the completion of the history of metaphysics. This culminated in the 1961 publication of Heidegger's two-volume (in English, four-volume) *Nietzsche*. The full unfolding of this trajectory, according to the standard narrative, terminates in Heidegger's embrace of *Gelassenheit*: "letting be." All of this is central to the familiar apologetics on Heidegger's behalf by his defenders as well as Heidegger's own self-apologetics (as laid out, for instance, in the famous *Der Spiegel* interview), and there is in fact considerable warrant for it in the texts. Did Nietzsche "ruin" him by contributing to the Nazi commitment in the first place or by making necessary the heroic labors of disengaging himself from that commitment (to the extent that Heidegger did disengage himself)? Possibly both.[63] It's clear from Heidegger's own account that Nietzsche helped to make him a Nazi.[64] For Heidegger, then, the critical distancing from Nazism necessarily took the form of a critical distancing from Nietzsche (which required a philosophical exertion of epic proportions). So cast within this framework, the question then becomes, When exactly did Heidegger liberate himself from the spell of Nazism and become an apostle of *Gelassenheit*?

So far so good. The truth, however, is that there are significant problems with this exculpatory narrative of

Heidegger's twin liberation from Nietzsche and Nazism. Consider the following:

1. He never relinquished his party membership.

2. As we know from Appendix A of Faye's book, Heidegger remained in the good graces of the regime, as documented by secret police files that testify to his continuing to be considered an exemplary Nazi, as defined by the regime (contrary to the story he told in 1945 and in 1966).[65]

3. In his January 20, 1948, letter to Herbert Marcuse, he could still say that it was his yearning for "spiritual renewal" that motivated his political commitment in 1933.[66] What a feat of hermeneutical imagination it was to interpret the seizure of power by a gang of racist thugs as an enhancement of spirituality!

4. In 1953, he could publish the suggestion that there had been such a thing as "the inner truth and greatness" of German fascism, even if the Nazis themselves *betrayed* that possibility of truth and grandeur.[67] This notorious line was reaffirmed and elaborated upon in Heidegger's 1966 *Der Spiegel* interview: "I see the situation of man in the world of planetary technicity not as an inextricable and inescapable destiny, but I see the task of thought precisely in this, that within its own limits it helps man as such achieve a satisfactory relationship to the essence of technicity. *National Socialism did indeed go in this direction* [my italics]. Those people, however, were far too poorly equipped for thought to arrive at a really explicit relationship to what is happening today and has been underway for the past 300 years." Even for the Heidegger of 1966, National Socialism in principle can be the source of that "satisfactory relationship to the essence of technicity"

that Heidegger seeks and that modernity in general puts out of reach. The problem is that the official political representatives of the movement ("those people")—or perhaps more likely, party ideologues who were in bitter competition with Heidegger—failed to understand themselves and their movement in a sufficiently Heideggerian manner. I don't think it would be going too far to say that according to Heidegger's own self-understanding (as expressed in this interview), his philosophical stance toward National Socialism (as an idea rather than as a regime) had not undergone any significant alteration between 1935 and 1966! One can draw the same shocking entailment from Heidegger's willingness in the *Der Spiegel* interview to defend his 1933 Rectoral Address: "Who among those who have engaged in polemics against this address has read it thoroughly, thought it through and interpreted it in terms of the situation of those times?"[68] Heidegger *could have said* to his interviewers, "I was talking nonsense. I was deluded." Instead, he stands by the Rectoral Address and excoriates his critics (as he did in the letter to Marcuse). This notorious Nazi text—intended to marry Hitler and Plato—was famously, and aptly, described by Otto Wacker, Minister of Culture and Education for Baden under the Nazi regime, as Heidegger's "private National Socialism."[69] I don't see how one can avoid inferring from the 1966 interview that it was a private National Socialism to which Heidegger remained committed long after 1933.

5. Near the end of his life, Heidegger decided to include the *Black Notebooks* (including explicitly racist passages conjuring up a diabolical conspiracy on the part of "world Judaism") in the official *Collected Works*, whereas any reasonably sane person would have burned

them, or at least burned the most incriminating passages. It's as if he either were trying to spur a revival of fascist ideology or intended to confess to the world just how grievously stained he had been by that ideology. All of this is thoroughly damning. Also fairly damning is a story related by Bambach.[70] Heidegger had a carved swastika decorating the stone well outside the window of his study in the cabin in Todtnauberg. According to a visitor at the ski hut (Rainer Marten), the swastika was removed at the conclusion of the war, *but no earlier.* As Bambach comments, "Heidegger retained an elemental faith in the symbolic power of the National Socialist myth . . . until 1945."

Even if one hadn't known in 1933 that the Nazis would launch a project of wholesale genocide in the 1940s, one surely couldn't avoid knowing *right from the start* that Nazism was a political movement founded on violence, dictatorship, and racial hatred. (Marcuse made this point in his letter to Heidegger dated May 12, 1948.) Heidegger bought into all of that and subsumed it under the rubric of "spiritual renewal"! Where was the truth and grandeur in any of that? It's not what any of us would associate with truth and grandeur—with or without extermination camps. Our conclusion: even a "best-case scenario" account of the history of Heidegger's philosophical development falls *far* short of an adequate exculpation.

***

As a sequel to our brief consideration in chapter 1 of Freud and Weber as intellectual heirs of Nietzsche, it may be of interest to resume that discussion in the context of our current treatment of Heidegger as an intellectual and political heir of Nietzsche. In chapter 1 I tried to suggest that Nietzsche offers a kind of *fetishism* of the tragic and the heroic. It is in precisely this sense that Heidegger is a direct disciple of Nietzsche. Of course, one could say something similar about Weber. But my sense with Weber is that for him the world *just is* tragic; this is part of what he intends when he speaks of polytheism as the "default position," so to speak, of human experience—hence it's less a question of "fetishizing" tragedy. Accordingly, my verdict on Weber would be much less harsh than my judgments concerning Nietzsche and Heidegger.

As I put it in an earlier section, for Heidegger (even though he never really spells this out in so many words), peasants, soldiers, and Romantic poets have a privileged access to the ineffable mystery of Being. Nietzsche, by contrast, doesn't particularly care about peasants or soldiers; all he really cares about, as he says in *Schopenhauer as Educator*, are "artists, philosophers, and saints," because they are capable, single-handedly, of putting human cultures on a different and higher plane. Nietzsche, no less than Heidegger, hates modernity and wants to see it disappear—because modernity's egalitarianism means that the welfare of shopkeepers and state functionaries counts for as much as that of great artists like Wagner and great philosophers like Schopenhauer. (Why great artists and great philosophers but not great scientists? Why Schopenhauer and Wagner but not Einstein? I don't think that there is a good answer to this question.)

Weber's view is more complicated: his view of modernity is as harsh as that of the harshest of modernity's critics (Theodor Adorno or Alasdair MacIntyre, say). Modernity is "an iron cage": it's hard to see that as a flattering description! But Weber, unlike Heidegger and Nietzsche, *affirms* modernity—for "dialectical" reasons, one could say. Living in the iron cage is a test of character and that appeals profoundly to Weber's tragic sensibility.[71] The worse modernity is, the more intense is the experience of tragic fate or tragic destiny and hence the greater the potentiality of nobility in "manfully" facing up to grim existential imperatives. (I would actually be inclined to say that because it doesn't rest upon the entertaining of fantasies about the transcendence of modernity, Weberian nobility is ultimately *more noble* than Nietzschean nobility.) So for Weber, precisely the unlovability of modernity makes it more lovable, or more redeemable. It's a bit like Nietzsche's amor fati, but applied to modern life.

Freud and Weber are *very pessimistic liberals*. Nietzsche and Heidegger are very pessimistic (about the existing dispensation) but also very hopeful/hubristic *antiliberals*. It's their hope/hubris that's dangerous! Freud and Weber aren't Nietzscheans, but they're *shadowed* by Nietzsche and especially by Nietzsche's critique of modern culture. (Weber, in "Science as a Vocation," says that only "overgrown children" would take seriously the idea of happiness as moderns conceive it in the wake of Nietzsche's "devastating" depiction of the last men.) All four of the thinkers that concern us here—Nietzsche, Freud, Weber, and Heidegger—are committed to conjuring up a deeper sense of tragic pathos than is made available by the rationalistic approach to life privileged by liberal modernity. For all four of them, life in liberal modernity involves a basically shallow and naive response to the world—which doesn't mean that all four want to banish it. Nietzsche and Heidegger do; Weber doesn't, for the reason I specified in

116

the previous paragraph; and Freud doesn't because (given Freud's deeply pessimistic account of human nature) the alternatives are guaranteed to be far worse. I'm certainly with Freud on this. Nietzsche was right that this whole intellectual movement was started by Schopenhauer, with his stringent rethinking of Western rationalism in the light of the unfathomable forces that are impenetrable by reason. And in that sense, Nietzsche's heirs are also Schopenhauer's heirs.[72]

Let me add one more point: One might say that for Weber and Freud science itself supplies the ethos of steely courage and cold-eyed realism that Nietzsche sought to introduce into philosophy. This whole pathos is captured by Weber's term "disenchantment," which Freud too fully buys into: it is precisely the man of science who exhibits the manliness, refusal to be duped by sentimentalism, and unflinchingness required to face up to the stern realities of life as they truly are. This indeed opens up an enormous philosophical chasm with Freud and Weber on the one side and Nietzsche and Heidegger on the other. Freud and Weber's debt to Nietzsche is beyond question. Yet Nietzsche wanted to unleash the life-affirming energies of Dionysus, whereas Freud wanted to rein in or domesticate the id (whether in the form of Dionysian Eros or Dionysian Thanatos) by appealing to the analytic powers of Logos and Weber wanted to look for possibilities of nobility precisely within a world where processes of rationalization reach their apogee.

Chapter 2

Heidegger's Icy Silence

HANNAH ARENDT: People ought to leave him in peace.
KARL JASPERS: I don't think it desirable "to leave Heidegger in peace." He is a presence, and one that everyone who wants an excuse for his own Nazi past likes to
fall back on. The significance of his behavior seems to
me of no small consequence for current politics in the
Federal Republic.[73]

In closing, let me come back to Gadamer and his determination to stand by Heidegger. In a TV documentary
entitled "The Magus of Messkirch," available on You-
Tube, Gadamer (with Jacques Derrida sitting next to him)
makes the following statement: "[The question was put to
me: 'you said] that Heidegger was so upset about Röhm
because he realized that his expectations regarding the
spiritual renewal of Europe were a mistake. So how come
he *didn't* get upset about the extermination camps that
were so much worse and so incredibly shameful for us?'
My reply was: he was so upset that he couldn't open his
mouth about it." Gadamer appears to say this in a tone of
considerable indignation that people dare to put this challenge to Heidegger.[74] This defense of Heidegger is quite
misguided on multiple levels: First, Gadamer parrots
Heidegger's own outrageous line that what drew him to
fascism and Hitlerism was the promise it offered of effect-
ing a "spiritual renewal" of Europe. Second, Gadamer
(again taking at face value Heidegger's own apologetics)
presumes that Heidegger fully realized his mistake at
the time of the Röhm purge. That was in 1934, whereas
we know for a fact that Heidegger's belief in Hitler and

Nazism extended until *at least* 1936 and probably much later. Third, Gadamer asserts that Heidegger was horrified and shamed by the extermination camps. We have good anecdotal reasons to be skeptical of this latter suggestion. Consider the following story told by Heidegger's friend, Rudolf Bultmann, about a postwar encounter between them: "'Now you must,' I said to him, 'like Augustine write retractions [*Retractiones*] . . . in the final analysis for the truth of your thought.' Heidegger's face became a stony mask. He left without saying anything further."[75] What we glean about Heidegger's character from the Bultmann story is reinforced by an account given in Hans Jonas's *Memoirs* concerning a 1969 visit by Jonas to his former teacher: "Any clarification on his part, let alone a word of regret, was not to be. What had come between us for good would remain shrouded in silence."[76] These stories help to put in context another story that was passed on to me and that rings true. Stanley Rosen informed his teacher Leo Strauss that he planned to go meet Heidegger. Strauss said words along the following lines: Fine, go have an intellectual discussion with him. But don't shake his hand.

Near the end of *The Periodic Table*, Primo Levi's masterpiece describing his experiences during the Holocaust as well as before and after the war, Levi gives an account of a postwar correspondence that he had with a German manager under whom he did slave labor in a chemical factory at Auschwitz. The German was not exactly a persecutor but was still tangibly stained by complicity with the Nazi terror. Levi imagines two kinds of letters that such a German, twenty years after the Nazi defeat, might write to a former concentration camp inmate: "a humble, warm, Christian letter, from a redeemed German; a ribald, proud, glacial letter from an obdurate Nazi."[77] Levi's point is that this particular German, a typically unimpressive but not outrightly evil human being, wrote letters that were neither one nor the other, thus illustrating the neither-black-nor-white character of human reality. *Not so with Heidegger.* Consider again the exchange with Marcuse. The second polar possibility sketched by Levi, the outrightly evil one, exactly describes Heidegger's tone with Marcuse: proud, glacial, obdurate. He had gained not a particle of humility, compassion, or wisdom from the Nazi catastrophe, as is clear to anyone who reads the Marcuse-Heidegger exchange. The recent *Black Notebooks* revelations have stoked up further waves of Heidegger controversy, but in essence they tell one nothing that one cannot infer from his arrogant, impenitent January 20, 1948, letter to Marcuse. Only a real Nazi, as opposed to a naïve fellow-traveler, could have written such a letter. In fact, Faye plausibly suggests that the whole enterprise of German revisionism spearheaded by Ernst Nolte in 1986–1987 is already latent in Heidegger's 1948 letter to Marcuse.[78] Hermeneutical generosity is generally an important intellectual virtue, but drawing together all the various troubling aspects of the Heidegger dossier surveyed above, we may well have reached the stage where we justly conclude that this particular philosopher—notwithstanding his intellectual greatness—just isn't worthy of that sort of generosity.

Conclusion

How to Do Theory in Politically Treacherous Times

> A succession of cycles and contingencies, history has no overall direction. But if any trend can be discerned at the present time, it is hardly favourable to the west. In part this is the normal course of history. The western pre-eminence of the past few hundred years was never going to be permanent. . . . As it faces an increasingly disordered world, the greatest danger for the west comes from the groundless faith that history is on its side.
>
> —John Gray

Many of us are reeling today. With the UK Brexit vote in June of 2016, it was evident that the populism genie was now fully out of the bottle, and suddenly something like the election of a demagogic Donald Trump was no longer beyond the realm of the possible. Indeed, it happened! What evil work would the genie next accomplish? Hence we seem to have been thrust into a new Zeitgeist that few of us anticipated or were prepared for.[1] If, as many claim about the Brexit vote, this is just an understandable reassertion of national sovereignty in a world that has globalized a bit too quickly and a bit too ambitiously for modern societies to cope with, perhaps this is not such a radical transformation of the political landscape in the Western world. And yet there are signs that something much darker and more ominous is unfolding. Especially with the election of Trump and his willingness to appoint an alt-right enabler as his chief strategist, the cultural-political shift seems to have been quite sudden, and many today are groping for intellectual or philosophical orientation in what seems to be a new world. "We are witnessing the birth of a new political order," as Steve Bannon himself puts it, and it does feel a bit like that. How do we interpret, first ideologically and then philosophically, what all of this may mean?

In 1989, Francis Fukuyama famously (and obviously quite prematurely) proclaimed the universal triumph of bourgeois liberal democracy.[2] Perhaps liberal democracy as it has developed in the West did not speak to all the multifarious longings of the human spirit. No matter; it had come out on top because all significant alternative ideologies either had been defeated or had run out of gas. Liberal democracy and the liberal-democratic way of life won out through a kind of process of elimination, through the self-discrediting of the most radical rival worldviews. Well, this "end of history," as Fukuyama called it, itself came to an end, as we all know, a mere twelve years later—on September 11, 2001—with the spectacular display by a jihadi ideology of its wholesale rejection of the liberal dispensation. Yet the revolt against Fukuyama's end of history did not end there. Today we see other radically illiberal ideologies coming out of the woodwork to threaten, root and branch, the moral-political world that we thought had been built on broad popular consensus. This crisis affects political philosophy as well. Leading philosophers of egalitarian liberal democracy such as John Rawls and Jürgen Habermas had presumed that the basic premises of liberal democracy were an established achievement built on a universal basis (a shared commitment to liberal justice in Rawls's case, a shared commitment to communicative reason in Habermas's case). They didn't say that it represented a Fukuyama-like end of history, but in effect that was implicit in their doctrines. If ferociously antiliberal views of life are still very much in play (and much of what we are seeing in contemporary politics would have to be a kind of optical illusion in order for us to think otherwise), the enterprise of contemporary liberal theory may have to be rethought at a deep level to take account of the manifestations of antiliberal backlash. In particular, the atrocious ideologies currently gaining ground in Europe and in other parts of the world are forcing us to reconsider what John Gray has called "the liberal delusion" (the faith that history favors liberalism).

In the brief reflections that follow, I want to elaborate a bit further on the suggestion already offered that there is a direct connection between the perils of end-of-history thinking, or the liberal delusion à la Gray, and the question of how to do theory. To simplify the argument, I'll restrict my discussion to three major philosophers of egalitarian liberalism: Rawls, Habermas, and Richard Rorty.[3] Of these three, Rorty was the one who was most explicit about his end-of-historyism: "Western social and political thought may have had the last *conceptual* revolution it needs."[4] According to the implicit philosophical horizon of Rawlsian and Habermasian egalitarian liberalism, we pretty much know what the moral and political truth is: it's liberal democracy and liberal egalitarianism as they are broadly understood in the present day. The history that got us to that moral outcome is irreversible. The most urgent task of theory is to clarify the policy details of that true moral vision, not to question whether and why the moral vision itself is the correct one. So we mainly preach to the converted: "we liberals" address fellow liberals. Of course, there are differences among us: we have different religious commitments, for instance. But we abstract from those differences and seek common ground as much as we can. We try not to get drawn into bedrock debate about "metaphysics" or ultimate commitments ("we try to bypass religion and philosophy's profoundest controversies," as Rawls puts it). Rawls's idea of "political liberalism" nicely captures this basic orientation or approach to the theory enterprise, but Habermas and Rorty, for instance, have their own ways of conveying the same fundamental purpose. Engaging with preliberal or transliberal moral and intellectual horizons is fairly pointless, since those other horizons have been historically superseded, deposited once and for all in the trash can of history. Hence for these three theorists (and countless others who pursue the project of liberal political philosophy), *history* rather than the making of a philosophical case seems to do most of the work—the heavy lifting—of establishing validity.[5] According to a Habermasian conception, this is supposedly a "sociological-historical learning process." That is, *history* delivers us to a new mode of experience and a new kind of rationality, *beyond metaphysical commitments*. But in fact there is no such thing. For Rawls, Rorty, and Habermas, Nietzsche has been refuted by history and sociology. He hasn't! He can only be refuted by a more compelling account of the human good. Privileging proceduralist morality (as Rawls and Habermas both do) is a way of saying that at bottom we're all liberals—which would be fine if it were actually true.

We don't know what the future will bring. The majority of people in Egypt today believe that Sharia should be the law of the land and that Egypt should be a theocratic state. That is, *piety* and not discursive or communicative equality should be the center of political existence. Who can guarantee that that view won't prevail a hundred years from now (or sooner)? And what happens to the Rawlsian-Habermasian appeals to procedural rationality and to pluralism as a sociological fact if it *does* prevail? Gray, in his critique of the liberal delusion, was right to challenge the presumption that history favors liberalism—that is, favors the idea of each individual having equal status in the conversation of one's society. These (largely unacknowledged) liberal philosophies of history cover over a lot of tacit liberal complacency. Human history is as much a process of *unlearning* as of learning!

By contrast to this "post-metaphysical" orientation common to Rawls, Rorty, and Habermas, I think that it's a big mistake to terminate the grand dialogue of visions of possible human life articulated throughout our theory canon. We need to retain our commitment to an enterprise of grand theory that doesn't presume that we've arrived, necessarily, at the final moral horizon and now just need to "tinker with the details" (as Hegel more or less suggested with respect to the modern *Rechtsstaat* once the French Revolution and Napoleon had legislated the broader moral horizon for modern existence). The grand horizons, from Plato to Machiavelli to Hobbes to Locke and Montesquieu to Nietzsche and Marx and Heidegger, are still in lively contention today. Reading these thinkers doesn't automatically turn us from liberals into something else (or hopefully it doesn't!); but hopefully what it does do is draw us into a fully ambitious questioning of what human life expects of us.[6]

Rawls and Habermas offer differing versions of this procedural liberalism but do it with similar motivation and in a similar spirit, one could say. As a citizen, I find their conceptions of civic life attractive: tolerant, oriented toward the encouragement of civic deliberation and mutual respect among people who share a political community, and oriented toward the encouragement of public-mindedness. Our political communities would certainly be better *as* political communities if they more fully embodied these liberal, egalitarian, and civicist ideals. But the practice of political philosophy that Rawls and Habermas stand for represents a kind of "fifth-wheelism" of philosophy. Rawls, Rorty, and Habermas presume that people who live in modern liberal polities already know what the ultimate political good is, and there's nothing that political philosophy can tell them that adds anything significantly new. It simply crystallizes the wisdom that liberal citizens already embody in their practice of citizenship: they deliberate with each other; they trade reasons and counterreasons; they presume that policies cannot be enforced without public justifications; and they treat each other as moral equals. If it's these procedures that embody the right moral philosophy and if everyone already knows that this is what a modern liberal democracy entails, why do we need philosophy? A completely "proceduralized reason," as Habermas conceives it, means that there is nothing further for philosophers to teach. Citizens in their procedural republic have already taught themselves all the essential moral truths. Yet this self-willed redundancy on the part of leading theorists of egalitarian liberalism will start to look fairly perilous if history surprises us (as it may well do) and keeps premodern and antimodern alternatives in vibrant contention with a liberalism that isn't universally received as attractive. In short, the dominant articulations of contemporary liberal theory strike me as variations on end-of-history philosophical complacency.[7]

Human beings, deprived of the possibility of philosophical reflection, fall short of their proper humanity. Whatever our crises may be (and let's face it, we currently face enormous political, cultural, and existential challenges that will not be easy to resolve with our current social, moral, cultural, and political resources), if those crises cause us to despair of casting theoretical or philosophical light on our darkness, the consequence will be not merely failures of praxis but, much more seriously, a diminished humanity. We cannot allow skepticism, cynicism, or political disillusionment to have that consequence. Being open to the possibility of philosophical reflection and philosophical dialogue, in any time and in any place, is what allows us to remain fundamentally hopeful as human beings. Political philosophy thrives in times of crisis (this is an old story in the history of the theory tradition!). Hence as our contemporary world gives some appearance of lurching into crisis, as citizens we may well have reason to despair; but as theorists (for those of us fortunate enough to be theorists), we have reason to anticipate a renaissance of political philosophy. So here's my proposal. We must read the great anti-liberal theorists—Rousseau, Marx, Nietzsche, Heidegger, and, yes, even Joseph de Maistre—*not* in order to appropriate them for liberal or leftist intellectual projects but in order to come to a deeper understanding of precisely why they turn their backs on bourgeois liberalism and hence why many of our fellow citizens are readily tempted to do the same. All the best theorists have, of course, always done this. But I'm inclined to think that, especially in recent decades, the confidence of the liberal West in the moral truth of the liberal-egalitarian dispensation and its idea of justice has duped theorists into thinking that this enterprise of radical and comprehensive philosophical dialogue is no longer essential.[8] Hopefully, the shock of the populist-nationalist backlash we are currently seeing will jolt theorists, intellectuals, and citizens into recognizing what often turn out to be tacit and unconscious end-of-history assumptions. As I hope is illustrated by the commentaries on Nietzsche and Heidegger presented in this book, an honest dialogue with these thinkers requires that we take them seriously without in any way liberalizing or whitewashing their most appalling and most illiberal ideas. If we fail to grasp what these enemies of the democratic Enlightenment are really saying, then we'll (deservedly) get sucker-punched by thinkers or doers less shy about taking them at their word.[9]

Again, the baseline for considering where we now stand is Fukuyama's declaration in 1989 that Western-style market-based liberal democracy had definitively prevailed over the alternatives. Friedrich Nietzsche may have been right or wrong in considering this epoch of hegemonic liberalism and individualism as a triumph of "the last man," but whether blessing or curse, the liberal dispensation is our fate, or so the end-of-history thesis had assured us. Such a pronouncement looks, today, very foolish indeed. To be sure, it can be perilous to make grand historical judgments from up close. We probably need a vantage point of decades or longer to really know whether Western liberal democracy is truly in crisis. But in 2017 it certainly looks as if a crisis (or interconnected series of crises) of fairly large proportions has begun or is at least on the horizon: Brexit in England; Trumpism in the US; Putinism in Russia and Orbánism in Hungary; Erdoğanism in Turkey; a real crisis of identity and purpose with respect to the whole EU project; the rise of a hypernationalist far right in various parts of Europe; a huge migrant crisis as a result of the chaos in the Middle East; a broad revolt against globalization; the challenge of militant Islamism, including a relentless stream of terrorist episodes, with escalating effects on all the other crises or perceived crises; and so on. No "end of history" in any of this! In a prescient July 2016 op-ed entitled "This Is Why Democrats Are Still Struggling," *New York Times* columnist David Brooks wrote, "Over the past few years, economic and social anxiety has metastasized into something spiritual and existential." I think that's right. (Brooks was talking about the US specifically, but I think his point can be generalized to liberal societies more broadly.)[10]

John Gray, in the essay I've already cited, rightly argues that for liberals, peace, freedom, and prosperity are self-evidently the natural aspirations of all human beings;

therefore, liberals get utterly bewildered when individuals or societies have the opportunity to choose these liberal ideals and instead unaccountably opt for antiliberal visions of life. According to Gray, we see this today quite clearly in Putin's Russia, where his authoritarianism and his reassertion of "the claims of geopolitics, ethnicity and empire" enjoy the strong support of millions of Russians.[11] As Russian opposition leader Boris Nemtsov put it in an interview with the *Globe and Mail* shortly before he was assassinated, "The most difficult question for Russia is what kind of revolution you will get—orange or brown or red. There is a very big danger for Russians and for the world because, unfortunately, nationalists and fascists are very popular in this country." This makes no sense to those for whom liberal ideals are the default aspiration of humanity. As we should have been taught by the catastrophes of the twentieth century, a cultural-economic-political crisis of the kind that we're currently experiencing provides the perfect opening for demagogues and lunatics who can exploit these crises in order to turn the whole world upside down. As a result, as Gray again points out, "across Europe, there has been a resurgence of the far right and the politics of hate";[12] and indeed there has. We are learning anew that fascism (including its theocratic versions), with its brown uniforms and black flags, has a romance that we liberals underestimate at our peril. Similar wisdom can be drawn from George Orwell as quoted by Graeme Wood in a powerful essay on the rise of ISIS written for *The Atlantic*: fascism is "psychologically far sounder than any hedonistic conception of life." Socialism and capitalism convey the following message: "I offer you a good time"; Hitler's message, by contrast, is "I offer you struggle, danger, and death." "We ought not to underrate [the latter's] emotional appeal."[13] As goes without saying, the relevance of this warning is not limited to the allure of ISIS.

It should seem obvious that the twentieth century is not something that any of us would want to replay in the twenty-first century. Nietzsche, in *Ecce Homo*, predicted in 1888 that the century to come would see "upheavals, a convulsion of earthquakes, a moving of mountains and valleys, the like of which has never been dreamed of. There will be wars the like of which have never yet been seen on earth." And so it came to pass! Why would any sane person want to do it all over again—namely, seeing the world convulsed by totalitarian ideologies, genocide, and apocalyptic wars? How can this prospect possibly be attractive in the eyes of contemporary adherents of the far right? Can human beings really be so blind and misguided as to have learned nothing from the twentieth century at its worst?

My bottom-line suggestion is that "we liberals" are in trouble if we take for granted that egalitarian liberalism is the final moral dispensation and hence spare ourselves the exertion of entering into dialogue with grand normative alternatives to twentieth- and twenty-first-century liberalism. We'll get blindsided by some radically nonliberal view of life because it turns out to have far more human appeal than we liberals have assumed or persuaded ourselves that it could have. As we've seen, that's already happening to us today! Author Damon Linker has put the key point quite well: "At both the academic (= Rawls) and public-intellectual (= Fukuyama) levels, discussion and thinking in the West has been dominated by centrist liberal managerialism for the past several decades. Now that's being challenged by virulent anti-liberals." So centrist liberal managerialism is unsatisfying. It's not inspiring enough. It doesn't move the soul. It's banal; it's a politics for the last man. Fine. And with what do we undertake to replace it? A regime of warriors and priests? A return from Enlightenment to magic? An appeal to the depths of the Volk (or Nietzsche's Pan-European successor to the Volk, whatever that might be)? Why be satisfied with what David Hume called "the calm sunshine of the mind" (which for him characterized the experience of Enlightenment morality) if we can insist upon a more bracing vision of life where the stakes are authentically life-and-death ones? Or where the unflinching confrontation with death promises a better-than-bourgeois authenticity, à la Heidegger? In *Thus Spoke Zarathustra* ("Zarathustra's Prologue," § 4), Nietzsche wrote, "I love the great despisers because they are the great reverers and arrows of longing for the other shore." Well, "the other shore" sounds good because, by definition, we have no idea what life will be like there. In the meantime, we are urged to put lots of energy into despising what perhaps doesn't meet Nietzsche's standards of grandeur yet almost certainly deserves more respect than it receives from him or those swayed by his rhetoric.

Nietzsche's formula of the death of God and Heidegger's formula of the forgetfulness of Being are two ways of articulating a shared intuition—namely, that there is a spiritual void at the heart of modernity. Needless to say, we don't want to deny ourselves the possible avenues of cultural self-reflection and self-criticism that are opened up by both diagnoses (or both versions of a shared diagnosis). But it is one thing to avail oneself of Nietzschean or Heideggerian insights into the spiritual deficiencies of modernity in a context where a commitment to liberal democracy is reasonably secure. It's something quite different to turn to Nietzsche or Heidegger for philosophical or cultural guidance in a context where that commitment is not fully secure or is actively insecure. The profound worry that has animated this book is the possibility that the context in which we currently find ourselves is the latter one.

As theorists, we must continually come back to Kant's immortal line: "Out of the crooked timber of humanity, nothing can ever be made straight." This is, alas, relevant to our vocation as theorists. If it is indeed true that human nature is permanently warped—a proposition for which there is vastly more historical evidence than we would care to acknowledge—then it follows that translations from theory to practice are more likely to be realizations of bad (or even evil) theory than of good theory.[14] Jason Jorjani, in a September 20, 2017, blog post explaining why he broke with Richard Spencer in the days following Charlottesville, lamented that the alt-right, which (in Jorjani's mind) was meant to be a grand project for a reborn aristocratic Aryan empire, had been turned by Spencer into "a magnet for white trash." Well, what on earth did he expect? Nietzsche might have voiced a version of the same risible complaint had he witnessed what the vulgar mob did with his idea of *große Politik* thirty-three years after his death. Again, I don't rule out the possibility that Nietzsche and Heidegger successfully articulate aspects of

spiritual or cultural vacuity in the liberal-egalitarian dispensation that defines modernity.[15] But what they offer by
way of new dispensations to supplant spiritless modernity
is *far worse*. One has to ask, Who ever gave us a guarantee that the problem of the human condition admits of a
solution?

Notes

Introduction

1. Quoted in an article by Jacob Siegel entitled "The Alt-Right's Jewish Godfather": http://www.tabletmag.com/jewish-news-and-politics/218712/spencer-gottfried-alt-right.

2. Similar sentiments have been voiced by a crackpot philosopher named Jason Jorjani who, from January to August 2017, entered into a well-publicized alliance with Spencer's organization. In a chilling video made available by the *New York Times*, Jorjani spoke of how he anticipated the creation of a new world order: "We will have a Europe, in 2050, where the banknotes have Adolf Hitler, Napoleon Bonaparte, Alexander the Great." See https://www.nytimes.com/2017/09/19/opinion/alt-right-white-supremacy-undercover.html?_r=0.

Also relevant here is Georg Lukács's interesting discussion of Nietzsche's critique of Bismarckian Prussia: Georg Lukács, *The Destruction of Reason* (London: Merlin Press, 1980), 340. Lukács quotes the famous celebrations of *große Politik* in *Beyond Good and Evil* and *Ecce Homo* and interprets these texts as saying that "Bismarck was not militaristic enough for Nietzsche." That is, Nietzsche was "criticizing Bismarck from the Right," hence anticipating fascism and *große Politik* as practiced by Hitler. That strikes me as a reasonable interpretation. Readers who fail to see Nietzsche's ardent desire for a return to a politics of empire are filtering out what Nietzsche really intends in these texts (a criticism that applies neither to Lukács nor to Spencer). In other words, Nietzsche deserves less credit for his repudiation of

German nationalism than many readers would assume, since it is not a liberal critique of nationalism but, on the contrary, an imperialistic critique of nationalism.

3. "Vladimir Posner Interviews Alexander Dugin," aired on Channel One (Russia), April 21, 2014: https://www.youtube.com/watch?v=tPkEDRSYUpo.

4. Anton Shekhovtsov, "The Palingenetic Thrust of Russian Neo-Eurasianism," *Totalitarian Movements and Political Religions* 9, no. 4 (2008): 491–506. The Dugin quotations are on pp. 501 and 503. In a recent book, Dugin similarly presents himself as the champion of "hierarchical, vertical, 'heroic,' and 'Spartan' values": Alexander Dugin, *Last War of the World-Island* (London: Arktos, 2015), 46.

5. For a fuller account of Dugin, see my essay "Russia's Ecumenical Jihadist," *Inroads*, no. 37 (Summer/Fall 2015): 92–100. The description of Nietzsche given by Bertrand Russell in chapter 1, note 2 may or may not be valid as an encapsulation of Nietzsche; it certainly *is* valid as an encapsulation of Dugin.

6. Charles Clover, *Black Wind, White Snow: The Rise of Russia's New Nationalism* (New Haven: Yale University Press, 2016), 159. On Evola, see Mark Sedgwick, *Against the Modern World: Traditionalism and the Secret Intellectual History of the Twentieth Century* (Oxford: Oxford University Press, 2004), chapters 5 and 9; and Nicholas Goodrick-Clarke, *Black Sun: Aryan Cults, Esoteric Nazism, and the Politics of Identity* (New York: NYU Press, 2002), chapter 3.

7. Cf. Lev Gumilev, as quoted at the top of p. 146 of Clover, *Black Wind, White Snow*. Also p. 239, citing Dugin's tendency to view "upheaval and violence less as a means to an end than as spiritual values in themselves." When Nietzsche wrote in *Twilight of the Idols*, "Skirmishes of an Untimely Man," § 38, "The free man is a *warrior*," it's hard to see why one shouldn't take this literally.

8. I actually sketch some of this very rhetoric, especially as Nietzsche deploys it in *The Antichrist*, in chapter 30 of my book *Civil Religion* (New York: Cambridge University Press, 2011). One should also check out how the Nietzschean rhetoric of "coddling" gets picked up by the young Leo Strauss, as discussed in my book *Political Philosophy: What It Is and Why It Matters* (New York: Cambridge University Press, 2014), 87. For one relevant source, see Nietzsche's reference to "European pampering" in *The Will to Power*, § 922.

9. Nietzsche, *The Will to Power*, § 872. The translation is quoted from Michael Scarpitti, "The Perils of Translation, or Doing Justice to the Text," 38: https://www.academia.edu/32250206/The_Perils_of _Translation_or_Doing_Justice_to_the_Text. The Scarpitti essay offers interesting discussion of alternative translations of this text; I have also benefited from personal correspondence with Scarpitti. Cf. *The Antichrist*, § 2: "The weak and the failures shall perish: first principle of *our* love of man. And they shall even be given every possible assistance." See also chapter 1, note 50.

10. Martin Heidegger, *Being and Truth*, trans. Gregory Fried and Richard Polt (Bloomington: Indiana University Press, 2016), 73; emphasis added. This was in the context of lectures delivered in the winter semester of 1933–1934 and hence predated the Final Solution by at least eight years.

11. See my essay "The Rise, and Apparent Fall, of President Bannon," *Inroads*, no. 41 (Summer/Fall 2017): 83–95; and Joshua Green, *Devil's Bargain* (New York: Penguin, 2017), 204–208. Bannon consistently denies that he is racist or an adherent of the alt-right, but the following *Huffington Post* story suggests otherwise: http://www.huffingtonpost.com/ entry/steve-bannon-camp-of-the-saints-immigration_us_58b75206 e4b0284854b3dc03.

To be sure, Bannon was able to survive the knife-fights in the Trump White House only until August of 2017. Still, one has to ask what it says about the politics of the contemporary era that a dubious character like Bannon was ever considered worthy of a powerful office in the West Wing.

12. Allan Bloom, *The Closing of the American Mind* (New York: Simon and Schuster, 1987), 222.

13. Geoff Waite, *Nietzsche Corps/e: Aesthetics, Politics, Prophecy, or, The Spectacular Technoculture of Everyday Life* (Durham, NC: Duke University Press, 1996), 2.

14. Ibid., 35. On p. 145 of the book, Waite bemoans the fact that Stanley Rosen's warnings about Nietzsche have gone unheard. And twenty-one years later, Waite's own warnings have gone unheard as well.

15. Ibid., 47.

16. Ibid., 51.

17. For a fuller account of Foucault, see Beiner, *Political Philosophy*, chapter 10.

18. Timothy Snyder, *On Tyranny: Twenty Lessons from the Twentieth Century* (New York: Tim Duggan Books, 2017), 71.

19. For a fuller discussion of Maistre, see Beiner, *Civil Religion*, chapters 25–27. As regards Nietzsche, a key text is *On the Genealogy of Morals*, First Essay, § 16. From Nietzsche's perspective, what the French Revolution represented was the overthrow by "the rabble" of "the last political nobility of Europe." See also Lukács's account of the early Nietzsche's understanding of what constitutes the "principal enemy"—namely, "liberalism"—characterized by Nietzsche as "a disease from which German life has had to suffer since the great French Revolution in particular": Lukács, *The Destruction of Reason*, 325–326. If one is to have any insight at all into Nietzsche's political philosophy, it is impossible to put too much emphasis on his stance toward the French Revolution as the foundation of modern egalitarianism.

20. Alexis de Tocqueville, *Democracy in America*, trans. Harvey C. Mansfield and Delba Winthrop (Chicago: University of Chicago Press, 2000), 675: "Equality is perhaps less elevated; but it is more just, and its justice makes for its greatness and its beauty."

21. Heinrich Heine, *On the History of Religion and Philosophy in Germany and Other Writings*, ed. Terry Pinkard (Cambridge: Cambridge University Press, 2007), 42. This thesis of the dependence of modern philosophy on foundations set by the Reformation encapsulated by Heine can easily by culled from texts by leading modern philosophers from Hobbes and Spinoza at one end to Kant and Hegel at the other end. All these landmark philosophers of modernity, it goes without saying, were supremely self-conscious about how modern philosophy built upon the initial revolution represented by the Reformation as indeed a kind of "logical conclusion." See, for instance, Karl Löwith, *From Hegel to Nietzsche* (New York: Columbia University Press, 1991), 34.

22. Again, *Genealogy of Morals*, First Essay, § 16, is a key text. Relevant in this context is Nietzsche's opposition between the Renaissance as the symbol of a fundamentally *aristocratic* moral world and the Reformation as the symbol of a fundamentally *democratic* political world. There are a great many other texts in Nietzsche that one could cite bearing on this theme, but one text that shouldn't be overlooked is the

important discussion in *The Antichrist*, § 61. Finally, let me stress that notwithstanding significant "Maistrean" aspects to Nietzsche's thought, there is of course an enormous philosophical gulf between these two great reactionaries, centering on their diametrically opposed stances toward Christianity. For a brief discussion pinpointing this difference, see Beiner, *Civil Religion*, 313, note 15, and 342.

23. *The Heidegger Controversy: A Critical Reader*, ed. Richard Wolin (Cambridge, MA: MIT Press, 1993), 162. The full phrase is "a spiritual renewal of life in its entirety"—*eine geistige Erneuerung des ganzen Lebens*. See also Beiner, *Civil Religion*, 397, note 9.

24. Spencer's "toward us" in this podcast calls to mind Bannon's own usage of "for us" in his celebrated statement that Trump is "a blunt instrument for us": http://www.vanityfair.com/news/2016/08/breitbart-stephen-bannon-donald-trump-master-plan. It's fairly clear who the first "us" is, somewhat less clear who the second "us" is. Obviously, the question of how the two us's relate to each other is a quite important one.

25. See also Graeme Wood's invaluable profile of Spencer: https://www.theatlantic.com/magazine/archive/2017/06/his-kampf/524505.

26. Let me again mention Jason Jorjani (see note 2). Here too we have an illustration of the perils of (in Francis Bacon's famous phrase) "a little philosophy." See Landon Frim and Harrison Fluss, "Aliens, Antisemitism, and Academia," *Jacobin*, March 11, 2017: https://www.jacobinmag.com/2017/03/jason-reza-jorjani-stony-brook-alt-right-arktos-continental-philosophy-modernity-enlightenment/.

27. See the diagram contained in this Facebook post by Andreas Umland (a leading scholar of Dugin): https://www.facebook.com/andreas.umland.1/posts/10210005073216892.

This is partly a joke and partly no joke at all. Spencer, by his own account, fashions himself a disciple of Nietzsche. Dugin has published no fewer than four volumes of commentary on Heidegger, with apparently more to follow. The first of these to be published in English has been published by Spencer's own neo-Nazi press, Radix. Spencer commissioned his wife, Nina Kouprianova, to translate this volume on Heidegger from the Russian. Further volumes from Dugin's Heidegger commentary will appear with Arktos, another fascist press that formed an official alliance with Spencer's organization in the midst of the alt-right hoopla in response to Trump's securing of the presidency. When one combines the Umland diagram with the remarks on Bannon that I have just quoted from the Spencer podcast, things start to look sinister.

28. Clover, *Black Wind, White Snow*, 229.

Chapter 1

1. Geoff Waite helpfully offers a roll call of European left-wing Nietzscheans. In Germany: the young Lukács "and virtually the entire Frankfurt School." In France: "virtually all French intellectuals," encompassing Gide, Valéry, Malraux, Camus, Bataille, Klossowski, Deleuze, Guattari, Derrida, Foucault, Baudrillard, and Virilio. Waite, *Nietzsche's Corps/e* (Durham, NC: Duke University Press, 1996), 535, note 12.

2. Aldous Huxley opined that "*Zarathustra* was written by a dyspeptic professor" who used his philosophy to get even with the world for his unsatisfactory digestion. For Georg Lukács, Nietzsche was the Ur-ideologist of imperialist reaction who for this purpose had to be "denazified" by liberal apologists like Walter Kaufmann: Lukács, *The Destruction of Reason* (London: Merlin Press, 1980), 343. Bertrand Russell made the provocative claim that the mad King Lear's proclamation, "I will do such things—what they are yet I know not—but they shall be the terror of the earth," constitutes "Nietzsche's philosophy in a nutshell." Russell, *History of Western Philosophy* (London: George Allen and Unwin, 1961), 734. Conor Cruise O'Brien says, "[It wasn't required of Nazis that they] engage in exegetical acrobatics in order to like him. On the contrary it is in order *not* to see him as a proto-Nazi that these acrobatics are required. . . . He was sometimes frightened himself, even this most daring of thinkers. Frightened of some travesty of his thought, he said, and the gentle Nietzscheans take comfort from this. Frightened, I think myself, of what he was actually saying, and of what his messages might effect when they reached minds which were as bold in action as he was bold in thought." O'Brien, "The Gentle Nietzscheans," *New York Review of Books*, November 5, 1970.

3. Tracy Strong, "Nietzsche's Political Misappropriation," in *The Cambridge Companion to Nietzsche*, ed. Bernd Magnus and Kathleen M. Higgins (Cambridge: Cambridge University Press, 1996), 126:

"Many of those—I include myself to some degree among them—who first took Nietzsche seriously in the 1960s and early 1970s found in him a voice for liberation, indeed for the transfiguration of the drab world which we then felt ourselves inheriting."

4. For discussion, see Hans Sluga, *Heidegger's Crisis: Philosophy and Politics in Nazi Germany* (Cambridge, MA: Harvard University Press, 1993), 179–186; the Hoffmann photograph is reproduced on p. 187. For another short commentary (including a challenge to Sluga's interpretation), see Max Whyte, "The Uses and Abuses of Nietzsche in the Third Reich," *Journal of Contemporary History* 43, no. 2 (2008): 191.

5. Another such act of statecraft was Hitler's presentation to Mussolini in 1935 of an edition of the works of Nietzsche: see Otto Pöggeler, *Friedrich Nietzsche und Martin Heidegger* (Bonn: Bouvier Verlag, 2002), 22.

6. Nicholas Goodrick-Clarke, *Black Sun: Aryan Cults, Esoteric Nazism, and the Politics of Identity* (New York: NYU Press, 2002), 202. See note 60 below.

7. Walter Kaufmann translates it as "large-scale politics" in the former text and as "great politics" in the latter text. The former is patently meaningless. Notwithstanding the anachronism, "fascist politics" (a politics of postliberal, postegalitarian *grandeur*) seems to capture much more faithfully what Nietzsche actually has in mind.

8. Nietzsche's letter to Franz Overbeck, dated October 18, 1888, is quite important (and fully consistent with everything Nietzsche conveys in his published works on these topics): a crucial aspect of why Nietzsche embraces an antinationalistic position is that German nationalism originally arose as a reaction against Napoleon—that is, against the Napoleonic project "to turn Europe into a political and *economic unit.*" Nietzsche did not write these lines as a prophet of the EU! Whatever *große Politik* might mean, it is presumably intended to be a resumption of the *imperial* promise of grandeur offered by Napoleon and defeated by Napoleon's defeat. As goes without saying, the liberal aspects of Napoleon's political project are of no interest to Nietzsche.

9. Richard J. Bernstein, *Beyond Objectivism and Relativism* (Philadelphia: University of Pennsylvania Press, 1983), 264 ("Appendix: A Letter by Professor Hans-Georg Gadamer").

10. Charles Bambach seems fully justified in situating Heidegger within a long German intellectual tradition centered on the trope

of opposing "the ideas of 1914" to "the ideas of 1789": Bambach, *Heidegger's Roots* (Ithaca: Cornell University Press, 2003), xxiv and 127–128, including note 38. Cf. Richard Wolin, "Preface to the 2016 Edition," in *The Politics of Being* (New York: Columbia University Press, 2016), xv. As textual evidence, consider two letters from Heidegger to Elisabeth Blochmann, dated June 22, 1932, and January 19, 1933, cited by Pöggeler on p. 5 of *Friedrich Nietzsche und Martin Heidegger*: as Nietzsche rightly perceived, liberalism is condemned "by virtue of its inability to appreciate 'rank order.'" Liberalism = "universal leveling" and the hegemonic rule of a deliberately willed mediocrity. The point of trying to recover Greek thought and Greek experience is to bring about "a new historical mission [*Auftrag*] and another beginning [*Anfang*]," thereby ushering in a new dispensation by which the "dwarfs" (*Gezwerge*) of present-day humanity can be "swept away" (*weggefegt*). See also chapter 2, note 61. As Pöggeler points out (6), the trope of a "dwarfed" humanity is drawn directly from Nietzsche (*The Use and Disadvantage of History for Life*, § 9). Pöggeler also cites (6) a letter of September 18, 1932, in which it seems to be suggested that *Being and Time* is the foundation stone of this mission and is therefore something far beyond a mere "book"; it is, rather, a civilizational project. For the actual letters, see Martin Heidegger and Elisabeth Blochmann, *Briefwechsel 1918–1969*, ed. Joachim W. Storck (Marbach am Neckar: Deutsche Schillergesellschaft, 1990), 52–54 and 57–58. It's implicit throughout these statements by Heidegger that "the ideas of 1789" did not represent moral progress for humankind but rather constituted a path to Nietzsche's last man. Moreover, I find it very hard to believe that Heidegger ever changed these views in any significant way.

11. *Ecce Homo*, "Why I Am a Destiny," § 1. Jeremy Fortier has drawn my attention to *The Gay Science*, § 38, where Nietzsche presents himself as a self-conscious seducer of the young and does so in a way that directly anticipates this self-image as "dynamite."

12. Julius Evola, *Ride the Tiger: A Survival Manual for the Aristocrats of the Soul*, trans. Joscelyn Godwin and Constance Fontana (Rochester, VT: Inner Traditions, 2003), 3.

13. Ibid., 4–5, 209.

14. Ibid., 118.

15. Ibid., 29.

16. Ibid., 173.

17. Ibid., 178, 174, 177.

18. Ibid., 178.

19. Ibid., 176.

20. Ibid. *Ride the Tiger*, originally published in 1961, does not lay out a political project; on the contrary, it expresses a resignation to "*apoliteia*" (detachment): 172–176. Still, this political resignationism clearly didn't preclude Evola from later urging on political extremists of the far right, as I flag in the next paragraph.

21. Ibid., 51.

22. Ibid., 6. Cf. 208–209, where Evola endorses Oswald Spengler's account of the transition from civilizations where "quality, spirituality, living tradition, and race prevail, to late and soulless urban forms in which the abstract intellect, economy and finance, pragmatism, and the world of the masses predominate, resting on a grandeur that is purely material." The latter are doomed to perish. Evidently Evola, like Heidegger, viewed fascism, and especially Nazism, as of superior "spirituality" relative to the alternatives—namely, communism and liberal democracy.

23. Goodrick-Clarke, *Black Sun*, 67–68.

24. Martin Heidegger, *Nietzsche*, Volume 3: *The Will to Power as Knowledge and Metaphysics*, ed. David Farrell Krell (San Francisco: Harper and Row, 1987), 4.

25. Thomas Mann, *Last Essays* (London: Secker and Warburg, 1959), 151.

26. Waite, *Nietzsche's Corps/e*, 212; cf. 232.

27. See *The Gay Science*, § 143. As Walter Kaufmann points out in his edition of the book, it is *the very first text* in which Nietzsche refers to the *Übermensch*. Yet in the same breath, Nietzsche also refers to *Untermenschen*. As regards *Gay Science*, § 143, Michael Scarpitti has made the interesting point to me that "demi-gods" is a plausible translation for *Übermenschen*, at least in this context. Cf. Emmanuel Faye, *Heidegger: The Introduction of Nazism into Philosophy*, trans. Michael B. Smith (New Haven: Yale University Press, 2009), 108.

28. Cf. Heidegger's reference to the modern West as "this moribund pseudocivilization"; *The Heidegger Controversy*, ed. Richard Wolin (Cambridge, MA: MIT Press, 1993), 38. It goes without saying that Nietzsche's influence was of *decisive* importance in Heidegger's coming to this view.

29. This is why, in chapter 30 of my book *Civil Religion* (New York: Cambridge University Press, 2011), I treat Nietzsche as a "civil religionist"—that is, as someone committed to the embrace of religion for reasons of utility rather than truth.

30. Both Nietzsche and Heidegger seem to be experimenting with the possibility of godless religions. Why would one be interested in reviving ancient religions or in inventing new religions if one believes (as both Nietzsche and Heidegger fairly clearly do) that theism is false? The implicit thought, so it would appear, is that the truth or falsity of theism is irrelevant. All that matters for them is the potential of such religions for generating existential depth (in Heidegger's case) or cultural grandeur (in Nietzsche's case).

31. Friedrich Nietzsche, *Untimely Meditations*, ed. Daniel Breazeale (Cambridge: Cambridge University Press, 1997), 63. Nietzsche pursues this same theme in a similar vein on pp. 67, 95, and 120–121.

32. "Spiritlessness" is a Nietzschean term at least insofar as R. J. Hollingdale uses it (ibid., 132) to translate *Mattherzigkeit*. Fainthearted-ness or feeble-heartedness are more literal translations, but spiritlessness isn't inaccurate.

33. Ibid., 148.

34. Lukács, *The Destruction of Reason*, 326.

35. *Basic Writings of Nietzsche*, ed. Walter Kaufmann (New York: Modern Library, 1968), 291. Nietzsche, on the same page, makes explicit that slavery is "*both in the cruder and in the more subtle sense* [my italics], the indispensable means of spiritual discipline and cultivation." Once again, Lukács is helpful in teaching us to take Nietzsche at his word, pointing out that central to Nietzsche's preoccupation with ancient Greece is "the idea that slavery is necessary to any real civilization" (*The Destruction of Reason*, 326–327). This is not a matter of Lukács's *interpretation* of Nietzsche; Nietzsche himself states it with utter clarity.

36. *The Portable Nietzsche*, ed. Walter Kaufmann (New York: Penguin, 1982), 543–544. This powerful text is quoted by Heidegger and implicitly endorsed by him, in Martin Heidegger, *What Is Called Thinking?*, trans. Fred D. Wieck and J. Glenn Gray (New York: Harper and Row, 1968), 67–68. Cf. Otto Pöggeler's commentary in "Heidegger's Political Self-Understanding," in *The Heidegger Controversy*, ed. Wolin, 207. As Pöggeler makes explicit, what Heidegger is really endorsing here

is Nietzsche's opposition between, on the one hand, "democratism" as "the decadent form of organizing power," and on the other hand, "tradition and authority" as it existed in, for instance, nineteenth-century Russia: "old Russia with its autocratic czars, the power of its nobility, its lack of bourgeois spirit (and its pogroms)."

37. Georg Simmel, *Schopenhauer and Nietzsche*, trans. Helmut Loiskandl, Deena Weinstein, and Michael Weinstein (Urbana: University of Illinois Press, 1991), 168.

38. Ronald Beiner, *Philosophy in a Time of Lost Spirit* (Toronto: University of Toronto Press, 1997), chapter 9.

39. *Basic Writings of Nietzsche*, ed. Kaufmann, 326. Cf. *The Will to Power*, § 144: "Moralities and religions are the principal means by which one can make whatever one wishes out of man, provided one possesses a superfluity of creative forces and can assert one's will over long periods of time." As this text states with crystal clarity, iron volition, uninhibited creativity, a ruthless ambition to reshape humanity, a willingness to instrumentalize religion, and a reorientation to dramatically longer temporal horizons are central to Nietzsche's basic project. Real cultures think in centuries, whereas with modern pseudocultures, as Nietzsche puts it in *Twilight of the Idols*, "one lives for the day, one lives very fast, one lives very irresponsibly."

40. *Untimely Meditations*, ed. Brezeale, 144; my italics.

41. Ibid., 192. Cf. 145: the philosopher = "the judge of life."

42. Ibid., 78; my italics.

43. Ibid., 79. A nice encapsulation of Nietzsche's argument is offered by Leo Strauss in his 1940 lecture, "Living Issues of German Postwar Philosophy": "historical knowledge, as self-knowledge of man, as *reflection*, is dangerous to spontaneity; human life and human history are essentially spontaneous; therefore, the total victory of historical consciousness, of history *understood*, would be the end of history itself, of history *lived* or *done*." Heinrich Meier, *Leo Strauss and the Theologico-Political Problem* (Cambridge: Cambridge University Press, 2006), 121; cf. 116–117. Strauss also highlights extremely well how Nietzsche's appeal to life against science crucially set the agenda for figures like Spengler and Heidegger. My thanks to Sophie Marcotte Chénard for bringing this interesting text to my attention.

44. *Untimely Meditations*, ed. Breazeale, 132–133.

45. The doctrine of eternal return is meant to debunk and supplant the Christian view that the world is purposive and upheld by a caring providence, and to divide humanity into those who can endure this severe new worldview and those who cannot. The doctrine of will to power is meant to give metaphysical sanction to those who, in Nietzsche's estimation, represent strength and self-affirmation.

46. See my discussion of the relevant Strauss-Löwith correspondence in *Political Philosophy: What It Is and Why It Matters* (New York: Cambridge University Press, 2014), 89–90.

47. Lukács puts it well when he sketches Nietzsche's characteristic "oscillation between the most acute feeling for nuance, the keenest oversensitivity, and a suddenly erupting, often hysterical brutality"—what Lukács also refers to as Nietzsche's "Jekyll-and-Hyde character": Lukács, *The Destruction of Reason*, 315.

48. *Basic Writings of Nietzsche*, ed. Kaufmann, 766.

49. Ibid., 728.

50. Ibid., 730. What Kaufmann translates as "relentless destruction" perhaps somewhat softens the ferocity of the German: *schonungslose Vernichtung*, or merciless annihilation. If Nietzsche means for us to take this seriously (and if he doesn't, it's hard to grasp what's the point of writing such things), one has to wonder just how many modern human beings, in Nietzsche's view, count for these purposes as other than degenerate and parasitical.

51. Cf. Waite, *Nietzsche's Corps/e*, 196: "*Pace* his many existentialist, postanalytic, and post-Marxist fans alike, Nietzsche had use neither for 'individuals' by themselves nor for 'radical pluralism.' His was always a full-bore *social* project."

52. *Basic Writings of Nietzsche*, ed. Kaufmann, 400.

53. Simmel, *Schopenhauer and Nietzsche*, chapter 8.

54. The "moralism" of Socrates and Plato, as Nietzsche sees it, is a crucial part of the story. But equally important is the *rationalism* of Socrates and Plato. Nietzsche, in his very first book, *The Birth of Tragedy*, personifies Schopenhauer's "representation" as Apollo and personifies Schopenhauer's "will" as Dionysus. According to the implicit Nietzschean narrative, a view of the world that privileges Apollo over Dionysus, pretending that the dark forces of mystery and unfathomableness can be rendered into rational clarity, is bound to be shallow. Both Socratic moralism *and* Socratic rationalism conspire against the

tragic depths of existence that potentially ennoble us. Heidegger (as we'll see in chapter 2) puts this in a different philosophical framework but draws a similar moral: the metaphysical tradition, inspired by Platonic rationalism, seeks rational apprehension/mastery of the world and hence loses touch with the primordial and unfathomable powers of "Being."

55. The same is emphatically the case with contemporary neofascist thought: see, for instance, Goodrick-Clarke, *Black Sun*, chapter 5.

56. Cf. *The Antichrist*, § 57: the enormous existential chasm separating the ancient Hindu caste system from anything that we would associate with "modern ideas" is precisely the mark of its being an embodiment of a normatively authoritative *natural* order.

57. It's worth noting that Kierkegaard had very similar views. See my discussion of this in my review of Hubert Dreyfus's *On the Internet*: *Bulletin of Science, Technology and Society* 21, no. 5 (October 2001): 409–411. See also related themes in my discussion on pp. 183–188 of *What's the Matter with Liberalism?* (Berkeley: University of California Press, 1992) as well as Geoff Waite, "Radio Nietzsche," in *Gadamer's Repercussions*, ed. Bruce Krajewski (Berkeley: University of California Press, 2004), 207–208, note 58.

58. Gita Mehta, *Snakes and Ladders: Glimpses of Modern India* (New York: Anchor Books, 1997), 120. Arundhati Roy, in *The God of Small Things* (New Delhi: IndiaInk, 1998), 73–74, similarly refers to a time "when Paravans were expected to crawl backwards with a broom, sweeping away their footprints so that Brahmins or Syrian Christians would not defile themselves by accidentally stepping into a Paravan's footprint."

59. See the text cited in note 34.

60. I taught an undergraduate course last year that included Nietzsche, and one of my students in his final essay, presumably without knowing what he was doing, quoted *The Antichrist* directly from a neo-Nazi website (www.nationalvanguard.org)! Similarly, Heidegger's "Rectoral Address" is available on a website called Aryanism.net.

61. Alexis de Tocqueville, *Democracy in America*, trans. Harvey C. Mansfield and Delba Winthrop (Chicago: University of Chicago Press, 2000), 675.

62. Ibid., 663.

63. In a letter to Leo Strauss dated July 13, 1935, Karl Löwith in effect suggests (though this is my gloss) that if Nietzsche had really achieved the liberation from ressentiment that he desired, his tone would approximate that of late antiquity (e.g., Stoicism)—namely, a pathos of accepting the world as it is and being at peace with it. There are moments when Nietzsche's writings achieve that. But overall, there's far too much hysteria in his texts (especially his late texts) to be able to claim the transcendence of resentment that for Nietzsche himself is a condition of nobility. For Löwith, this is the mark of Jacob Burckhardt's decided superiority to Nietzsche.

64. Karl Jaspers, *Tragedy Is Not Enough*, trans. H. A. T. Reiche, H. T. Moore, and K. W. Deutsch (London: Victor Gollancz, 1953), 38–39.

65. Beiner, *Political Philosophy*, xxxviii, note 11. The whole of the second prologue (xxix–lv) is an attempt to make an extended case for Freud and Weber as heirs of Nietzsche. It is no accident that Weber, in one of only two explicit references to Nietzsche in "Science as a Vocation," zeroes in on what he sees as Nietzsche's valid insight that it is merely a Platonic prejudice to assume that there is a metaphysical harmony between, for instance, beauty and goodness; see Max Weber, *The Vocation Lectures*, ed. David Owen and Tracy B. Strong (Indianapolis: Hackett, 2004), 22.

66. Friedrich Nietzsche, *The Will to Power*, ed. Walter Kaufmann (New York: Vintage Books, 1968), 242 and 232.

67. *Untimely Meditations*, ed. Brezeale, p. 136.

68. Weber, *The Vocation Lectures*, 22. Rodney Livingstone's translation referring to "the elder Mill" makes it sound as if Weber is referring to James Mill (John Stuart Mill's father), but Peter Lassman has pointed out to me that Weber really means "late Mill"—that is, the later works of John Stuart Mill and the *Three Essays on Religion* in particular.

69. Max Weber, *Political Writings*, ed. Peter Lassman and Ronald Speirs (Cambridge: Cambridge University Press, 1994), 75–79.

70. Ibid., 77.

71. Max Weber, *The Religion of India: The Sociology of Hinduism and Buddhism*, ed. Hans H. Gerth and Don Martinale (New York: Free Press, 1958), 169. Cf. the Nietzschean idea of providentialist theology as "pampering" or "coddling" as cited in the introduction, note 8.

72. William Christian, *George Grant: A Biography* (Toronto: University of Toronto Press, 1993), 281. There's another interesting

Strauss anecdote in the same biography (and an interesting contradiction between the two anecdotes). Grant apparently asked Strauss when would he most like to have lived, and Strauss replied: "Now . . . because only now would I have available to me the greatest philosophic statement of antiquity in Plato, and its most profound denial in Nietzsche" (293). If, as Strauss had preferred, Nietzsche had never published his dangerous ideas, then of course Strauss would be denied the Nietzsche side of the Plato-Nietzsche dialogue that, for Strauss, made it worthwhile to be living in late modernity.

73. *Selected Letters of Friedrich Nietzsche*, ed. Christopher Middleton (Chicago: University of Chicago Press, 1969), 227; I have modified Middleton's translation. Berel Lang, in "Misinterpretation as the Author's Responsibility (Nietzsche's fascism, for instance)," in *Nietzsche, Godfather of Fascism? On the Uses and Abuses of a Philosophy*, ed. Jacob Golomb and Robert S. Wistrich (Princeton: Princeton University Press, 2002), 47, attributes this line to a letter from Nietzsche to his sister, but Middleton, on pp. 227–228, explains that this supposed letter was a forgery by Elisabeth based on the letter to von Meysenbug. Nietzsche goes on, "Yet that is the *torment* [*die Qual*; my emphasis] of every great teacher of mankind: he knows that, given the circumstances and the accidents, he *can* become a disaster as well as a blessing to mankind." Cf. Stanley Rosen, *The Ancients and the Moderns: Rethinking Modernity* (New Haven: Yale University Press, 1989), 205: "As the initiator . . . of the destruction of Western bourgeois society, does not Nietzsche also guarantee the vulgarization of his own works? Will he not come to life as a self-constructed Frankenstein?" The sentences that Nietzsche wrote to von Meysenbug might be interpreted as his own anticipation of the questions posed by Rosen.

Chapter 2

Note to epigraph: Stanley Rosen, *The Question of Being: A Reversal of Heidegger* (New Haven: Yale University Press, 1993), xii.

1. *The Marx-Engels Reader*, 2nd ed., ed. Robert C. Tucker (New York: W. W. Norton & Co., 1978), 90. I owe this good quote to Ed

Andrew. Jean-Paul Sartre famously (and rightly) declared, "Heidegger has no character" ("A More Precise Characterization of Existentialism," in *The Writings of Jean-Paul Sartre*, ed. Michel Contat and Michel Rybalka [Evanston: Northwestern University Press, 1974], vol. 2, 156). However, it should be noted that Sartre made this claim in the context of an attempt to insulate Heidegger's *philosophy* from contamination by Heidegger's complicity in National Socialism. I believe that this was a gigantic mistake on Sartre's part.

2. Emmanuel Faye, *Heidegger: The Introduction of Nazism into Philosophy*, trans. Michael B. Smith (New Haven: Yale University Press, 2009). The original French edition of the book was published in 2005. Two years before that, another important book no less damaging to the reputation of Heidegger's philosophy was published in the US: Charles Bambach, *Heidegger's Roots: Nietzsche, National Socialism, and the Greeks* (Ithaca: Cornell University Press, 2003). See also *Reading Heidegger's "Black Notebooks 1931–1941,"* ed. Ingo Farin and Jeff Malpas (Cambridge, MA: MIT Press, 2016).

3. *Reading Heidegger's "Black Notebooks 1931–1941,"* ed. Farin and Malpas, 24. "Frankfurt" is a reference to the critical theory of the Frankfurt School.

4. Fred Dallmayr, *The Other Heidegger* (Ithaca: Cornell University Press, 1993), 3.

5. For one telling case in point (namely, the Heideggerian neofascism of Aleksandr Dugin), see the section to follow as well as my essay cited in the introduction, note 5.

6. Alexander Dugin, *Martin Heidegger: The Philosophy of Another Beginning*, trans. Nina Kouprianova (Arlington, VA: Radix, 2014), 168–175.

7. Ibid., 170; cf. 161–165. "Planetary idiocy of liberalism" is a good encapsulation of the view of modernity shared by Nietzsche, Heidegger, and Evola.

8. Ibid., 172–173. For an indispensable discussion of this intellectual-ideological milieu, see Leo Strauss, "German Nihilism," *Interpretation* 26, no. 3 (Spring 1999): 353–378. It suffices to check out the website of Arktos Media (the main English-language publisher of Dugin) to see that these thinkers (especially Schmitt) still command a significant following on the far right. Arktos has been described as "the biggest alt-right publishing company in the world": http://www

.thedailybeast.com/articles/2016/12/05/the-french-ideologues-who -inspired-the-alt-right.html. On July 12, 2017, Jason Jorjani, who at that point was editor-in-chief of Arktos though he quit soon thereafter, posted a letter on the Arktos website in which he singled out Heidegger as a key source of inspiration for contemporary fascists. Another far-right outfit of the same ilk explicitly lays claim to Heidegger as part of the fascist pantheon: http://www.counter-currents.com/2015/09/ remembering-martin-heidegger-5/.

9. Dugin, *Martin Heidegger*, 172. With respect to philosophy, "another beginning" (i.e., a replaying of the experience of Being associated by Heidegger with the pre-Socratic philosophers) becomes possible when Western philosophy reaches its end with Nietzsche (169). Heidegger's "another beginning" is simultaneously philosophical and cultural/political.

10. Ibid., 173; cf. 174–175.

11. "Fascism—borderless and red," in *Fascism Past and Present, West and East*, ed. Roger Griffin, Werner Loh, and Andreas Umland (Stuttgart: ibidem-Verlag, 2006), 508. My strong hunch is that Dugin's jarring line about the unprincipled pragmatism of "actually existing fascism" accords extremely well with Heidegger's own view about what went wrong with Hitlerism.

12. "Heideggerian and Apocalyptical Thinker: Alexander Dugin on Martin Heidegger": http://www.4pt.su/en/content/heideggerian -and-apocalyptical-thinker. The interview was conducted by Michael Millerman.

13. Dugin consistently claims that he is fully opposed to racism of any kind (and indeed insists that liberals, qua cultural imperialists, are the true racists). Dugin's links to (for instance) American neo-Nazis justify skepticism on this score: http://www.thedailybeast.com/meet-the -moscow-mouthpiece-married-to-a-racist-alt-right-boss.

Moreover, when I first became interested in Dugin, I watched on YouTube a video of a short talk he gave in Indonesia a few years ago (a video since deleted from YouTube). In it, Dugin no less than three times refers to the contemporary world order (pre-Trump) as "Pax Judaica." It is evident that no one other than a committed anti-Semite would deploy this ugly trope. In all likelihood, Dugin is faithful to the theory of "spiritual racism" articulated by Julius Evola (as opposed to garden-variety biological racism), and a broadly similar account works for Heidegger as well. For a relevant discussion, see: https://www.theatlantic.com/international/archive/2017/02/julius-evola-alt-right/517326/.

14. See note 11.

15. Faye, *Heidegger*, 30–31, cites evidence of Heidegger's political embrace of "the movement" in 1931–1932. Bambach, *Heidegger's Roots*, 31–38, makes clear that this political commitment developed out of an intellectual embrace of Nietzsche and Ernst Jünger starting in 1929–1930. Heidegger's relationship to the Nazi regime from the late 1930s onward is complicated, and Heidegger himself does much to cover up or obscure aspects of that relationship, but as I discuss in the penultimate section of this chapter, it would be wrong to think that he had fully detached himself from it, intellectually or politically, prior to the actual end of the regime in 1945.

16. See the last section of this chapter.

17. As I point out in note 2 of the introduction, one should not rush to the conclusion that Nietzsche's rejection of German nationalism is to Nietzsche's credit. Whether it is to his credit or not depends on the standpoint from which he criticizes (mere) nationalism. Dugin too, it should be recalled, claims to reject nationalism—ultimately, because his ultranationalism requires a politics of empire.

18. Hannah Arendt once referred to the relationship between Heidegger and his wife as "the alliance between mob and elite": *Within Four Walls: The Correspondence between Hannah Arendt and Heinrich Blücher 1936–1968*, ed. Lotte Kohler (New York: Harcourt, 2000), 189. This characterization of the Heidegger marriage fails to acknowledge that the alliance between mob and elite was housed within Heidegger's own soul.

19. There's an interesting line in a letter from Hannah Arendt to her husband, Heinrich Blücher. Arendt writes, "Heidegger . . . simply can't keep away from mass movements"; ibid., 324. The context here was the German antinuclear movement of the late 1950s (a very different kind of politics from the "mass movements" of the 1930s, needless to say). Still, it offers an intriguing possible glimpse into an aspect of Heidegger's personality that was obviously in deep tension with his rhetoric about "the they," the "publicness [that] obscures everything," and so on.

20. Martin Heidegger, *Being and Time*, trans. Joan Stambaugh (Albany, NY: State University of New York Press, 1996), 219–246. All in-text citations to follow are from this edition.

21. Martin Heidegger, *The End of Philosophy*, trans. Joan Stambaugh (New York: Harper and Row, 1973), 1.

22. Martin Heidegger, *Schelling's Treatise on the Essence of Human Freedom*, trans. Joan Stambaugh (Athens, OH: Ohio University Press, 1985), 22.

23. Martin Heidegger, *Early Greek Thinking*, trans. David Farrell Krell and Frank A. Capuzzi (New York: Harper and Row, 1975), 78. Cf. Julius Evola, *Ride the Tiger*, trans. Joscelyn Godwin and Constance Fontana (Rochester, VT: Inner Traditions, 2003), 27, on the need to display "the particular type of evasion and anesthetization, on the part of a humanity that has lost the meaning of existence." See also p. 30 ("internal anesthetization or prophylaxis, aimed at evading the problem of an existence robbed of any meaning") and p. 34 ("a system of anesthetics and surrogates"). It's plausible to think that both Heidegger and Evola are picking up a basic trope in Nietzsche, even if Nietzsche didn't use the exact term *anesthetization*. Whether he did or not, it's certainly a Nietzschean line of thinking. (Clearly, the crowd of last men in the parable of the madman are anesthetized, or self-anesthetized, in relation to the cultural crisis that they are living.)

24. Samuel Scheffler, *Death and the Afterlife* (Oxford: Oxford University Press, 2013), 44.

25. Ian McEwan, *Enduring Love* (London: Vintage, 1998), 177.

26. Here is a five-word encapsulation of *Being and Time*: Søren Kierkegaard meets Immanuel Kant. Or (in slightly more than five words), *The Concept of Dread* meets the *Critique of Pure Reason*. Putting it that way should already make clear why *Being and Time* is an intrinsically tension-ridden philosophical exercise, prompting later revisions to Heidegger's way of doing philosophy.

27. See note 38 below.

28. Cf. the line about "the narcotization of anxiety in the face of thinking" quoted above from *Early Greek Thinking*. See also the phrase "dread in the face of dread": Martin Heidegger, *The Question Concerning Technology and Other Essays*, ed. William Lovitt (New York: Harper and Row, 1977), 112.

29. Paul Auster, *Leviathan* (New York: Penguin, 1992), 134: "Every hour of every day, people are dying when they least expect it. They burn up in fires, they drown in lakes, they drive their cars into other cars, they fall out of windows. You read about it in the paper every morning,

and you'd have to be a fool not to know that your life could end just as abruptly and pointlessly as any one of those poor bastards."

30. Martin Heidegger, *An Introduction to Metaphysics*, trans. Ralph Manheim (New Haven: Yale University Press, 1959), 46.

31. Richard Rorty, *Philosophy and Social Hope* (London: Penguin, 1999), 197.

32. See William McNeill, "The Descent of Philosophy: On the Nietzschean Legacy in Heidegger's Phenomenology," in *Nietzsche and Phenomenology*, ed. Andrea Rehberg (Cambridge: Cambridge Scholars Publishing, 2011), 103–120. McNeill also discusses Heidegger's significant appropriation of themes from the second Untimely Meditation in § 76 of *Being and Time*. In particular, Heidegger endorses Nietzsche's view that—in Heidegger's formulation—"historiography tends to alienate Dasein from its authentic historicity." Moreover, Heidegger devoted an entire lecture course to this particular work in 1938–1939. For a full discussion of the latter, see Mark Sinclair and Ullrich Haase, "History and the Meaning of Life: On Heidegger's Interpretations of Nietzsche's *2nd Untimely Meditation*," in *Heidegger in the Twenty-First Century*, ed. Paul J. Ennis and Tzirvanis Georgakis (Dordrecht: Springer, 2015), 65–81. These lectures by Heidegger have recently been published in English: Martin Heidegger, *Interpretation of Nietzsche's Second Untimely Meditation*, trans. Ullrich Haase and Mark Sinclair (Bloomington: Indiana University Press, 2016).

33. Leon Wieseltier, "Among the Disrupted," *New York Times Book Review*, January 18, 2015.

34. Martin Heidegger, *Basic Writings*, ed. David Farrell Krell, rev. ed. (London: Harper Perennial, 2008), 220. All in-text page references to follow are from this edition. See Anson Rabinbach, "Heidegger's 'Letter on Humanism' as Text and Event," in Rabinbach, *In the Shadow of Catastrophe* (Berkeley: University of California Press, 1997), 97–128, for a good discussion of how the *Letter* represents a "combination of philosophical and strategic considerations" (99). Perhaps offering another indication of the *Letter*'s strategic dimension, Faye, *Heidegger*, 246, draws our attention to an enigmatic note in which Heidegger himself suggests that the *Letter* "ne parle jamais qu'à mots couverts" (never expresses itself in anything other than veiled formulations): Martin Heidegger, *Questions I* (Paris: Gallimard, 1987), 310. In any case, let me cite Rabinbach's ultimate judgment (for which there is compelling

evidence in the text): "The 'Letter' is a gesture of defiance in the cloak of humility" (115).

35. See, for instance, Günther Stern (= Günther Anders), "On the Pseudo-concreteness of Heidegger," *Philosophy and Phenomenological Research* 8, no. 3 (March 1948): 337–371. Anders was the first husband of Hannah Arendt and also a cousin of Walter Benjamin; in Germany he came to be a famous intellectual in his own right. Like other tough critics of Heidegger such as Karl Löwith, Hans Jonas, and Herbert Marcuse, Anders had been a student of Heidegger's in the 1920s. There are a lot of good lines in Anders's critique of Heidegger, but here's the one that I like best: "One is tempted to vary the famous French [saying] 'ni homme ni femme, c'est un capucin' into: 'ni homme, ni capuchin, c'est un Dasein'" (349). In a similar vein, Faye (*Heidegger*, 299) writes that Heidegger's appeals to the truth of Being, bordering on the occult, lack all determinacy, hence are "elusive enough to appear unscathed by criticism and mysterious enough for everyone to read into it whatever they were looking for." On pp. 98–101 of Martin Heidegger, *Nature, History, State 1933–1934*, ed. Gregory Fried and Richard Polt (London: Bloomsbury, 2015), Peter E. Gordon points to the dangers of presuming, as Heidegger certainly did presume, that one possesses a privileged phenomenological method that penetrates to and captures authentic concreteness, relative to which all other ways of doing philosophy merely offer abstractions.

36. Nietzsche and Heidegger disagree in their normative assessments of the Renaissance (see the introduction, note 22). Heidegger sees it as part of the genealogy of modernity and as such condemns it. Nietzsche, by contrast, sees it as representing the kind of grandeur and epic human possibilities squelched by modernity. (Burckhardt's influence on Nietzsche is relevant here.)

37. For essential historical contextualization concerning Heidegger's preoccupation with Hölderlin, see Bambach, *Heidegger's Roots*, 241–246; and Faye, *Heidegger*, 103–112. This cult of Hölderlin is inseparable from Heidegger's yearning for the replacement of Christianity by some kind of neopagan worldview (for which there is a clear precedent in Nietzsche, obviously). By far the best discussion of all this is Hans Jonas, "Heidegger and Theology," in Jonas, *The Phenomenon of Life* (Chicago: University of Chicago Press, 1966), 235–261; Jonas's main point is that Christian theologians who entertain naïve hopes about

engaging a theologically relevant dialogue with Heidegger's philosophy grossly underestimate the depth of his hostility toward Christianity. This theme is bound to be extremely worrying as soon as one reflects on the parallel project of repaganization palpably present in Nazism as well as contemporary versions of neofascism. Consider, for instance, the following discussion of the propagan, anti-Christian views of Julius Evola: https://www.theatlantic.com/international/archive/2017/02/julius-evola -alt-right/517326/.

38. Whenever one encounters the word "uncanny" (*unheimlich*) in English translations of Heidegger, it's very important to keep in mind its etymological connections with *Heimat* and *heimlos*, which get lost in the English. I owe this helpful point to Ed Andrew. See also Martin Heidegger, *Nietzsche*, Volume 4: *Nihilism*, ed. David Farrell Krell (San Francisco: Harper and Row, 1982), 226, where Heidegger conjures up the notion of Being as "mystery" (*Geheimnis*). Here, too, we have the same root.

39. See the important discussion of Nazi themes in Heidegger's seminar devoted to Hölderlin during the 1934–1935 winter semester: Faye, *Heidegger*, 103–112; cf. 86. See also the discussion of "politically charged" philosophical categories highlighted by Faye on p. 6 of his book; it ought to be noticed that categories of this kind are particularly prominent precisely in the sections of the *Letter of Humanism* that celebrate Hölderlin over against the metaphysical tradition that Heidegger is determined to challenge. I don't think that it's going too far to speak of a "Nazi spillover" from the explicitly Nazi seminars of 1933–1935 to the text of 1946. (Faye himself goes much further: he sees the Nazi dimensions of Heidegger's thought originating in the 1920s and encompassing the totality of Heidegger's work, from start to finish.) Jean Beaufret, the addressee of the *Letter on Humanism*, notoriously went on to become a Holocaust denier (Faye, 312), so it's possible to say that the *Letter* was compromised at both ends, so to speak.

40. Cf. Heidegger, *Nihilism*, ed. Krell, 248: "the homelessness of historical man within beings as a whole."

41. What Karsten Harries writes on pp. 211–212 of *Reading Heidegger's "Black Notebooks 1931–1941,"* ed. Farin and Malpas, concerning the centrality of this theme in Heidegger is particularly powerful.

42. Geoff Waite, "On Esotericism," *Political Theory* 26, no. 5 (October 1998): 603–651 at p. 630.

43. Bambach, *Heidegger's Roots*, 327, suggests that the *Letter on Humanism*'s "anti-nationalism," such as it is, is to some extent strategic; cf. 328.

44. Martin Heidegger, *Nietzsche*, Volume 1: *The Will to Power as Art*, ed. David Farrell Krell (San Francisco: Harper and Row, 1979), 220. See also Faye, *Heidegger*, 108.

45. "Gadamer on Strauss: An Interview," interview by Ernest L. Fortin, *Interpretation* 12 (1984): 11.

46. Why do I say that the *Letter* discloses a politics that is "perhaps somewhat duplicitous"? Look at the discussion of nihilism on pp. 249–250. Heidegger claims indignantly that the nihilism with which he is tarred by his critics is purely "invented" and denies that his repudiation of humanism entails "a defense of the inhuman." But the nihilism and inhumanity of the Nazi regime from 1933 to 1945 are a historical reality, not an invention; and Heidegger's enthusiastic embrace of Nazism implicated him in that nihilism, even if his enthusiasm waned considerably in the later years of the regime. Hence Heidegger's grand tone of having been unjustly slandered strikes me as disingenuous.

47. Heidegger, *An Introduction to Metaphysics*, 16.

48. This judgment is made explicit in Martin Heidegger, *Hölderlin's Hymn "The Ister,"* trans. William McNeill and Julia Davis (Bloomington: Indiana University Press, 1996), 54–55. Addressing his students in 1942, Heidegger denounces America's entry into World War II, opining that it is incapable of participating in history—because America as such is defined by "historylessness" (*Geschichtslosigkeit*). (Interestingly, the same trope of historylessness occurs in one of Heidegger's viciously anti-Semitic texts in the *Black Notebooks*.)

49. Needless to say, the Heidegger industry is of such gargantuan proportions that there is virtually bound to be an industry of Heidegger apologetics of equally large proportions. For a very good account of the relevant perils (namely, the perils of overinvestment in such a deeply compromised thinker), see Martin Woessner's excellent *Los Angeles Review of Books* review of Peter Trawny's *Freedom to Fail: Heidegger's Anarchy*: https://lareviewofbooks.org/review/fail-slow-fail-hard-heidegger.

50. Leo Strauss, "Living Issues of Postwar German Philosophy," in Heinrich Meier, *Leo Strauss and the Theologico-Political Problem*, trans. Marcus Brainard (Cambridge: Cambridge University Press, 2006), 125.

51. Chapter 5 of Bambach, *Heidegger's Roots*, offers an authoritative analysis of the manipulations practiced by Heidegger on his Nietzsche lectures of 1936 to 1945. What I refer to as the doctoring of Heidegger's texts, Bambach—equally aptly—calls "a philosophical cover-up" consciously "engineered" by Heidegger (267; cf. 248). See also p. 253: "a strategy of elision and omission," "a choreographed effort"; p. 254, note 13: "a self-conscious practice of political cleansing"; and Geoff Waite, *Nietzsche's Corps/e* (Durham, NC: Duke University Press, 1996), 152–153 and 405, note 50.

52. See note 22.

53. Martin Heidegger, *Schellings Abhandlung über das Wesen der Menschlichen Freiheit*, ed. Hildegard Feick (Tubingen: M. Niemeyer, 1971), 28.

54. Martin Heidegger, *Schelling: Vom Wesen der menschlichen Freiheit*, ed. Ingrid Schüßler (Frankfurt am Main: Vittorio Klostermann, 1988) [GA 42], 40–41.

55. Heidegger, in a letter to Marcuse dated January 20, 1948, writes that his lectures and courses *from 1933 onward* were "unequivocally" anti-Nazi, to the extent that they actually inoculated his students against Nazi ideology, and that this would be demonstrated if they ever came to be published: *The Heidegger Controversy*, ed. Richard Wolin (Cambridge, MA: MIT Press, 1993), 163. We of course now know that such claims were blatantly untrue.

56. Martin Heidegger, *Nietzsche: der Wille zur Macht als Kunst*, ed. Bernd Heimbüchel (Frankfurt am Main: Vittorio Klostermann, 1985) [GA 43], 193.

57. *The Heidegger Controversy*, ed. Wolin, 110: "It may be that it will take 300 years for [the thought or insight that Heidegger aims at] 'to have an effect.'" By implication, it took three hundred years for the disaster of modernity to come to fruition (cf. *Der Spiegel* interview: "underway for the past 300 years"), hence it is not unreasonable to expect it to take just as long for this disaster to be undone. Also, Bambach, *Heidegger's Roots*, 300: "preparations of those decisions that confront the West in this and in the coming century"; and the Heidegger letter quoted by Bambach on p. 311: "awaken[ing] the Germans to their innermost calling . . . only after a century has passed." Even more alarmingly, see Heidegger as cited in Waite, *Nietzsche's Corps/e*, middle of p. 386. Heidegger's insistence on

thinking in centuries is also highlighted by Richard Wolin in "National Socialism, World Jewry, and the History of Being," *Jewish Review of Books* (Summer 2014): https://jewishreviewofbooks.com/articles/993/national-socialism-world-jewry-and-the-history-of-being-heideggers-black-notebooks/.

As is helpfully pointed out by Stanley Corngold and Geoffrey Waite, this trope of ideas being activated only after three hundred years of dormancy is borrowed from Nietzsche: "A Question of Responsibility: Nietzsche with Hölderlin at War, 1914–1946," in *Nietzsche, Godfather of Fascism? On the Uses and Abuses of a Philosophy*, ed. Jacob Golomb and Robert S. Wistrich (Princeton: Princeton University Press, 2002), 197.

58. *Heidegger, Philosophy, and Politics: The Heidelberg Conference*, ed. Mireille Calle-Gruber (New York: Fordham University Press, 2016), 40–41; cf. 46.

59. See note 69.

60. One also cannot rule out that Habermas was alluding to Gadamer's roots in the Stefan George Circle, or to possible evidence of Gadamer having been personally compromised vis-à-vis the Nazis. For a disconcerting discussion of the latter, see Geoff Waite, "Salutations," in *Gadamer's Repercussions*, ed. Bruce Krajewski (Berkeley: University of California Press, 2004), 256–306.

61. See Martin Heidegger, *Being and Truth*, trans. Gregory Fried and Richard Polt (Bloomington: Indiana University Press, 2016), 71 and 129 for especially explicit statements by Heidegger of his principled rejection of all universalism. In the first text, Heidegger speaks of the task of a resumption of the Greek inception of philosophy as "the deepest necessity of our German Dasein"—a task that requires that "the fundamental possibilities of the proto-Germanic ethnic essence" be drawn upon and brought to mastery. In the second text, Heidegger characterizes Plato's doctrine of ideas as the origin of "the conception of the human being [defined by] *rational being in general*." "In the Enlightenment and in liberalism, this conception achieves a definite form. Here all of the powers against which we must struggle today have their root." I owe these important references to Ed Andrew. See also, in a similar vein, Martin Heidegger, *What Is a Thing?*, trans. W. B. Barton and Vera Fink (Chicago: Henry Regnery, 1967), 39.

62. Hans-Georg Gadamer, "Heidegger und Nietzsche: Nietzsche hat mich kaputtgemacht!", *Aletheia* 9/10 (1996): 19; cf. *The Cambridge Companion to Gadamer*, ed. Robert J. Dostal (Cambridge: Cambridge University Press, 2002), 261.

63. Heidegger apparently suffered three nervous breakdowns over the course of his life, the second of which coincided with his discovery that Nietzsche was not a resource for counternihilism but himself the expression of the deepest nihilism. See Otto Pöggeler, *Friedrich Nietzsche und Martin Heidegger* (Bonn: Bouvier Verlag, 2002), 14 and 16. Pöggeler clearly interprets "kaputtmachen" as a reference to this second nervous breakdown, which he intimates involved suicidal aspects.

64. Ibid., 5–6; and Pöggeler, "Heidegger, Nietzsche, and Politics," in *The Heidegger Case*, ed. Tom Rockmore and Joseph Margolis (Philadelphia: Temple University Press, 1992), 132–133. For the texts highlighted by Pöggeler, see chapter 1, note 10.

65. After quoting from this report that Heidegger maintained a regular subscription to the official Nazi newspaper, Faye pointedly remarks, "Now you have to have examined one day in your life a copy of the *Völkischer Beobacter* to understand what it might mean to receive and read such a newspaper daily in one's home" (Faye, *Heidegger*, 326–327).

66. *The Heidegger Controversy*, ed. Wolin, 162.

67. Heidegger, *An Introduction to Metaphysics*, 199. For evidence of Heidegger's mendacity with respect to the contentious sentence, see Jürgen Habermas, "Work and Weltanschauung," in Habermas, *The New Conservatism*, ed. Shierry Weber Nicholsen (Cambridge, MA: MIT Press, 1989), 161–163. Heidegger had three assistants begging him to remove the offending line, which he adamantly refused to do. As a concession to them, he inserted the famous parenthesis about "the encounter between planetary *Technik* and modern man," later pretending that this parenthesis had been in the original 1935 lecture and apparently destroying evidence that it hadn't.

68. *The Heidegger Controversy*, ed. Wolin, 95; cf. 162.

69. Bambach, *Heidegger's Roots*, 82.

70. Ibid., 271.

71. See Ronald Beiner, *Political Philosophy: What It Is and Why It Matters* (New York: Cambridge University Press, 2014), lii, note 26.

72. See chapter 1, note 54; cf. Strauss, "German Nihilism," 361, where Strauss refers to Schopenhauer as the start of what came to fruition in Nietzsche. Nietzsche's debt to Schopenhauer is obvious, even if it leads eventually simply to a set of inversions: Schopenhauerian repudiation of and desire to transcend or be liberated from the will, inverted, becomes Nietzschean reveling in assertions of the willing self; Schopenhauerian compassion flips over into Nietzschean anticompassion; the theme (in Schopenhauer) of what is life-negating, inverted, becomes the theme (in Nietzsche) of what is life-affirming; Schopenhauer's wanting redemption from sin, inverted, becomes Nietzsche's wanting liberation from the consciousness of sin; and so on. It might also be worth noting that Nietzsche's ideas of the *Übermensch* and the eternal return are both anticipated by Schopenhauer: Arthur Schopenhauer, *The World as Will and Representation*, Volume 1, ed. Judith Norman, Alistair Welchman, and Christopher Janaway (Cambridge: Cambridge University Press, 2014), 212 ("*übermenschlichen Wesens*"), 310 (affirmation of life "of endless duration, or of perpetually new recurrence"), and 350 ("doing it all again"). My overall judgment, I think, is that Nietzsche's appropriation of Schopenhauer makes Schopenhauer look very sane and sober by comparison. In the case of Freud, see the detailed discussion in Christopher Young and Andrew Brook, "Schopenhauer and Freud," *The International Journal of Psychoanalysis* 75, no. 1 (February 1994): 101–118.

73. Hannah Arendt and Karl Jaspers, *Correspondence 1926–1969*, ed. Lotte Kohler and Hans Saner (New York: Harcourt Brace Jovanovich, 1992), 628 and 629.

74. See *Heidegger, Philosophy, and Politics*, ed. Calle-Gruber, 45, where the originator of the challenge is identified as Hilde Domin, an important German-Jewish literary figure. In a 1986 interview, Gadamer gave a strikingly different account of Heidegger's silence concerning Nazi evil. Asked why he thought Heidegger rebuffed all pleas (including pleas by Gadamer himself) to issue a *mea culpa* concerning his behavior under the Nazis, Gadamer offered the following thoroughly damning explanation: "My principal conviction on this point is that *Heidegger still remained sufficiently a Nazi after the war that he was convinced that world opinion was totally dominated by Jews*, and hence that anything he said would be turned against him." *Hans-Georg Gadamer on Education, Poetry, and History*, ed. Dieter Misgeld

and Graeme Nicholson (Albany, NY: State University of New York Press, 1992), 11; my italics.

75. Victor Farías, *Heidegger and Nazism*, ed. Joseph Margolis and Tom Rockmore (Philadelphia: Temple University Press, 1989), 282. What we get in this Bultmann story is indeed icy silence. But Emmanuel Faye seems to me fully justified when he writes, "Much has been said about Heidegger's 'silence' with respect to the annihilation of European Jewry by the Nazis. In reality, he did not keep silent, and what he expressed is far worse than silence" (Faye, *Heidegger*, 302). Considering Heidegger's letter to Marcuse, his *Der Spiegel* interview, and other tendentious accounts by Heidegger of his behavior, his "silence" is something more like mean-spirited intransigence.

76. Hans Jonas, *Memoirs*, ed. Christian Wiese, trans. Krishna Winston (Waltham, MA: Brandeis University Press, 2008), 193. A more famous, and more legend-enshrouded, encounter took place between Paul Celan and Heidegger in the Black Forest in 1967. There is much speculation that Celan experienced something very similar to what Jonas experienced; but unlike the Jonas story, it cannot be documented by anything spoken or written by Celan (apart from a poem that's open to a range of interpretations).

77. Primo Levi, *The Periodic Table*, trans. Raymond Rosenthal (New York: Schocken Books, 1984), 218.

78. Faye, *Heidegger*, 310.

Conclusion

Note to epigraph: John Gray, "The Liberal Delusion," *Prospect*, October 2014, 45.

1. Paul Berman, in his essay "The Counter-Revolution," *Tablet*, March 7, 2017, has helpfully given a name to this sense of a major historical sea change: http://www.tabletmag.com/jewish-news-and-politics/226761/the-counterrevolution. On April 20, 2017, just as I was completing my initial draft of this book, the Nietzsche scholar Babette Babich tweeted, "There is manifestly no phronesis [practical wisdom]

left in the world." It's tough to beat that as a nine-word encapsulation of our current situation.

2. Fukuyama's account was a popularized version of a thesis originally given wide currency by Alexandre Kojève, who in turn drew it from Hegel. The basic idea is that once the drama of history has conducted us to the final moral truth of freedom, equality, and universal recognition, at the most fundamental level there is in principle nothing further for historical action to accomplish. Nietzsche's polemic against Hegel in *The Use and Disadvantage of History for Life* should have prompted Kojève (and Fukuyama too, I guess) to expect an antiliberal backlash. Cf. Christopher Walker, "How Anti-Democratic Propaganda Is Taking Over the World," *Politico Magazine*, March 3, 2017: "In contrast to inward-leaning democracies, which have an 'End of History' sense of complacency, today's autocrats are vibrant internationalists in the ideas sphere.... The autocrats' toolkit now is used to actively compete on the democracies' home turf." See http://www.politico.com/magazine/story/2017/03/anti-democratic-propaganda-beijing-moscow-214858. This rightly conveys the warning that it can be politically dangerous to buy into end-of-history conceptions. Again, that's something that we could have learned from Nietzsche.

3. For a full discussion of all three, see chapters 9, 13, and 14 of my book *Political Philosophy (New York: Cambridge University Press, 2014)*.

4. Richard Rorty, *Contingency, Irony, and Solidarity* (Cambridge: Cambridge University Press, 1989), 63. It doesn't seem to me entirely accidental that Rorty published this sentence in the same year that Fukuyama published his famous article. However, as many have noted, Rorty was also the one who, to his credit, most clearly predicted Trump: *Achieving Our Country* (Cambridge, MA: Harvard University Press, 1998), 75–107.

5. A good example is Rawls's appeal to "the fact of reasonable pluralism" characteristic of modern liberal societies. The implication seems to be that this "fact" is sociologically irreversible, but actually it's eminently reversible. In principle, if a majority within such a society becomes convinced that moral homogeneity is normatively superior to moral pluralism, they can undo the fact of reasonable pluralism simply by expelling, or severely marginalizing, minorities responsible for the unwelcome heterogeneity. We are seeing something like that process of reversal in the "de-liberalization" in various societies that previously

appeared committed to political and cultural liberalism and existential pluralism. That is, the people composing such majorities need *normative* reasons to remain faithful to liberal pluralism.

6. Among theorists, there has been a bit of a backlash against Rawlsian and Habermasian normative theory—a backlash expressed in the so-called realism (versus "moralism") movement within recent political theory. This seems to me rather misguided. The proper response to shortcomings in contemporary normative theory, I would say, is to become more ambitiously normative rather than less so.

7. Again, recall Christopher Walker as quoted in note 2. Or consider the following remarks in a similar vein written by Owen Bennett-Jones: "Much of the Western commentary on the ascent of the Islamic State has been strikingly defensive. . . . Obama and Cameron have condemned the Islamic State's barbarity but—in contrast to the rhetoric of Bush and Blair—they haven't spoken passionately about the virtues of the West. . . . Surely the West should be able to articulate confidence in its precious values of tolerance and equality before the law": "When Jihadis Win Power," *London Review of Books*, December 4, 2014, 3. According to Bennett-Jones's interpretation, this reticence is directly related to a global decline in Western power. But even if this thesis of shrinking control were correct, it's far from clear why it would entail an inability or reluctance to articulate what the West stands for with respect to positive normative conceptions.

8. In the fall of 2016, I participated in a graduate seminar taught by my friend and colleague, Joe Carens. At one point in the discussion, Carens argued that the purpose of reading, say, Marx is not to confront the possibility that liberal justice is mistaken (we all know that it's true) but to incorporate Marxian insights concerning inequality in the cause of reflecting on how liberal thinking about equality and justice can be better perfected. In other words, we don't attempt to enter into the full radicalism of Marx's philosophical challenge to liberal thought but simply appropriate him for our own purposes. I would say that this is to make the same kind of mistake in relation to Marx that so many liberal and radical readers of Nietzsche and Heidegger make in relation to Nietzsche and Heidegger. It's a constriction or short-circuiting of what the most ambitious kind of theorizing should be.

9. *Beyond Good and Evil*, preface: the fight against Christianity "has created in Europe a magnificent tension of the spirit the like of

which had never yet existed on earth: with so tense a bow we can now shoot for the most distant goals." Yet "the democratic enlightenment" (= "freedom of the press and newspaper-reading") serves to "unbend this bow," thereby frustrating this longing of the European spirit. Nietzsche is speaking here both for himself and for Heidegger as well as for all partisans of the ultraright up to the present day. We know that Heidegger, right until the end of his life, was never won over to the virtues of democracy: see *The Heidegger Controversy*, ed. Richard Wolin (Cambridge, MA: MIT Press, 1993), 104; and the 1974 letter to Heinrich Petzet quoted in Thomas Sheehan, "Heidegger and the Nazis," *New York Review of Books*, June 16, 1988, 38. Martin Heidegger, *What Is Called Thinking?*, trans. Fred D. Wieck and J. Glenn Gray (New York: Harper and Row, 1968), 66–68, offers another telling instance of postwar (1954) Heideggerian polemicizing against democracy—invoking Nietzsche as a crucial authority on the deficiencies of a democratic culture. Nietzsche's project, writes Heidegger, is "to clear the field for the great decisions," and he makes emphatically clear that these decisions are out of reach as long as liberal democracy remains the reigning political order in Europe. "What did the Second World War really decide? . . . This world war has decided nothing," wrote Heidegger (66), meaning that any historical outcome that leaves liberal modernity intact counts for nothing. Hence the defeat of European fascism was of no consequence (!) because it left the spiritual emptiness of modernity just as it was.

10. In the essay cited in note 1, Berman writes, "As everyone has always recognized, liberalism does not address the profound questions of life. Liberalism prefers to leave questions of meaning to other people to answer." But insofar as this tends to leave people with the feeling of "a spiritual void," many of them start to hunger for the sense of legislated purpose supplied by radical forms of illiberalism. It doesn't take very much reflection to see that there's something importantly in common between this analysis and Nietzsche's.

11. Gray, "The Liberal Delusion," 40 and 42.

12. Ibid., 42.

13. Graeme Wood, "What ISIS Really Wants," *The Atlantic*, March 2015: http://www.theatlantic.com/features/archive/2015/02/what-isis -really-wants/384980/.

This is related to the vital issue, discussed in earlier chapters, of why thinkers like Heidegger, Carl Schmitt, and Evola see fascism as "spiritual" in a way that liberal democracy and communism supposedly aren't. The idea here, presumably, is that liberal-capitalist and socialist or communist societies can't see beyond physical longevity and material betterment (concerns that define Nietzsche's last man). Fascism, according to this highly questionable line of thinking, puts more on the line and hence offers the prospect of exalting "spirit" over "matter."

14. Cf. Charles Clover, *Black Wind, White Snow* (New Haven: Yale University Press, 2016), 5, where he describes his work on Eurasianist ideology as "a book about why bad ideas win out over good ideas, or at least better ones" and refers back to Dostoevsky's *Crime and Punishment* as "a meditation on how theory produces monsters."

15. Nicholas Goodrick-Clarke, *Black Sun: Aryan Cults, Esoteric Nazism, and the Politics of Identity* (New York: NYU Press, 2002), 70, summarizing a short essay of Evola's entitled "American 'Civilization,'" put the gist of Evola's argument like this: "Americanism" is an insidious project "to transform the world into an enormous suburban shopping mall." Obviously, one doesn't need to be an über-fascist like Evola to see this as a problem.

Acknowledgments

Four friends encouraged me to publish my recent pre-occupations as a book—namely, Lou Pauly, Ryan Balot, Sophie Marcotte Chénard, and Ed Andrew (to whom I also owe the Yeats epigraph that heads the introduction). They nudged, and I succumbed—hence this book, for which I owe them very warm thanks. I'd also like to thank Jeff Kopstein, whose solidarity and sharp wit has helped sustain me through some pretty grim reflections. Finally, I'm grateful to Damon Linker for his strong support of this project.